Death is a constant in this fallen world, ~ as we awaken to every new day. Tears can be the gentle rain on the fields of our future, or they can become our undoing.

What happens if we lose someone so close to us that we immediately find we just cannot function without them? Well, we either discover that we were more capable than we thought, or we allow ourselves to shrink back and give up, forgetting that our destinies were always intended to be eternal – as were our purposes.

To me it was an amazing adventure to watch Judy pick up the pieces after the death of her husband, Alan. With the old pieces that shattered her dreams, she designed a new infrastructure that was a blessing to all – including herself. Of course there was the pain. We all have that. How we deal with that pain, however, defines who we are on this earth and how we will be known in heavenly places. That will be our "new name."

In her book, Judy sets forth some very practical, Spirit-filled strategies that will enable the bereaved soul to rise to its highest – then one day look back in joy and victory. Discouragement and defeat will never be a part of our vocabulary again, except to help others.

This book is a "must read" for all.

Peter Scott Snyder, BA, MA, Ph.D.
(Missionary to China)

Widowhood is an epidemic, especially among older women. *A Widow's Might* is a very personal story through one woman's journey but is applicable to everyone. Judy shows us how widowhood is not the end, but can be the beginning of a wonderful new life, one in which the relationship with God can flourish. Many books about widowhood are about handling the loss, whereas Judy focuses on thriving in this new stage of life. There are blessings to be gained through the loss. Even during the health crisis of her husband, which ultimately led to his death, Judy found blessings from God each day – even in small things like getting help with her windshield wiper from a stranger. Sprinkled with Scripture, *A Widow's Might* is an honest, sometimes painful, but ultimately triumphant journey. Because I work primarily with elderly patients, I will recommend this book to those facing widowhood.

Kris Gallegos
MS, RN, APN, Senior Nurse Practitioner

In Judy's book, *A Widow's Might: The Secret to Finding Strength in God*, Judy demonstrates how a relationship with God helps us overcome the challenges we face in daily life and apply the principles of God's Word. Her joy and confident trust in God show us how we can walk in victory through an intimate relationship with Jesus Christ.

Pastor Lawson Perdue
Senior Pastor, Charis Christian Center, Colorado Springs, Colorado, Host of *Grace for Today* Television Program (TBN Network)

Starting to read *A Widow's Might,* I was caught up in the experiences of the writer. She communicated her feelings so well that it also became my reality. Her spiritual growth as the book progresses allowed even me to feel closer to God. I can sympathize with Judy's position as the situation with Alan's health deteriorates. However, women who are newly widowed, going through the grief process or, like Judy, waiting for the eventuality will find this book a great deal of comfort and a meaningful way to deal with grief. Learning to find yourself through God and depending on Him in all things is the powerful message of this wonderful book.

Donna Jensen
M.A. English Education, University of Maryland

I just finished reading Judy's wonderful book, but it is so much more than a mere book. It has opened my eyes, and I can hardly wait to start spending time with our God again on a more regular basis. I see and understand what I'm missing. Thank you, Judy, for allowing us to read your marvelous journey with our precious Father God. I want to buy copies for my family and friends! I want to share your story and God's goodness. Thank you again for giving us the opportunity to read your story.

Florence Lila
Accounting Specialist, Lake County, Illinois, Health Department

A Widow's Might is much more than a memoir of losing a husband. It goes beyond one experience to offer readers a real step forward on a spiritual journey to deepen their connection with God. Whether through sorrow, facing the unknown, or simply living day-to-day, this book puts forward insight and practical ways to enrich your faith and become more intimately acquainted with God.

Maureen Lang
Author of *The Oak Leaves,* Winner of Romance Writers of America's Golden Heart Award

I have discovered through the years that there are few books that truly reach out and grab people in their spirit. Judy's book, *A Widow's Might,* is one of those books. Her transparency on the painful and difficult journey she was thrust into will encourage and challenge many – and not just those who are going through a similar journey of losing a loved one. Her words will inspire many who feel hope slipping away, as they are struggling to face the seemingly insurmountable realities before them.

As I read each chapter, I was challenged time and again to simply pause and allow the Holy Spirit to speak to me about the situations of my life. I am thankful for Judy's faithfulness and obedience to put her pen to the trials and challenges that she faced, not alone, but with God's loving and powerful help. Allow her journey from "mite" to "might" to bring encouragement and light to the dark corners of your difficult path. You will discover, as she did, that God's love and power will bring you through – and to destinations you had never dreamed possible.

Steven R. Abbott
Lead Pastor, Epicenter Church, Gurnee, Illinois

A Widow's Might

A Widow's Might

The Secret of Finding Strength in God

Judy A. Knox

ANEKO
PRESS

Visit Judy's website: www.judyaknox.com

A Widow's Might – Judy A. Knox

Copyright © 2015

First edition published 2015

Cover Design: Amber Burger

Cover Photography: Andrew Mayovskyy/Shutterstock

Vignette: kisika/Shutterstock

Editors: Gloria Graham, Sheila Wilkinson

Printed in the United States of America

Aneko Press – *Our Readers Matter*™

www.anekopress.com

Aneko Press, Life Sentence Publishing, and our logos are trademarks of Life Sentence Publishing, Inc.

203 E. Birch Street

P.O. Box 652

Abbotsford, WI 54405

RELIGION / Christian Life / Death, Grief, Bereavement

Paperback ISBN: 978-1-62245-316-0

eBook ISBN: 978-1-62245-317-7

10   9   8   7   6   5   4   3   2   1

Available where books are sold

Share this book on Facebook:

Contents

To Doug and Julie and their families, who lived through all the struggles and frustrations with me; to Carol Sue, whose help was above and beyond the call of sisterly duty; to Mark, whose many kindnesses will never be forgotten; and to Kim, who so selflessly shared Mark with me during that time of need. Without all of your help and encouragement, I wouldn't have come through my trials with a story worth writing.

Acknowledgements

To all of my friends and family members, thank you for providing encouragement along the way.

In particular, I would like to thank my daughter, Julie Dahlberg, for all of her good advice. She preceded me in the pursuit of writing and introduced me to her Christian writers' group.

This book could never have been completed without the help of my writers' group, especially Maureen Lang, Jane Steen, Sherri Gallagher, Myra Wells, Tonja Brice, and Kris Long. Their thoughtful chapter-by-chapter input sharpened my skills and vision, resulting in a much more readable finished product.

My sister, Carol Sue McKenzie, also encouraged me and did a great job of proofreading. My friend JaVette Hall, whose careful proofreading caught many technical errors, provided invaluable insight. She understood what I was trying to say and helped me find the right way to say it.

Without the help of all these people, I would still be sitting on my sofa saying, "Some day I ought to write a book."

And I want to thank my publisher, Jeremiah Zeiset of Aneko Press, who believed that my message was worth sharing and provided the opportuntity to share it. Like a shepherd, he carefully watched over each step of the publishing process and patiently encouraged me to stay on task. I thank God for introducing me to this man who made the path to becoming a published author an exciting adventure instead of an arduous uphill struggle.

Introduction

On January 14, 2012, a month before our fifty-first anniversary, my husband was rushed to the hospital and underwent major heart surgery. During the next ten weeks he was in the Intensive Care Unit (ICU) where we lived through a series of ups and downs. As I turned to God in this frightening situation, I discovered that my walk with Him had been very superficial. Drawing close to Him as never before, I experienced His presence in a fresh, deeper, and more intimate way.

After ten weeks my husband died, but during that time I found God's peace that passes understanding and His perfect love that surpasses all comprehension and casts out all fear. God transformed me from a very fearful person, dependent upon my husband, to a strong woman who learned to trust in Him.

As I embarked on my life as a newly singled-out woman, I discovered the fullness of joy that comes only from lingering in God's presence. His joy became my strength. My new journey has been an adventure-filled time with God, where He is still teaching me to walk in the principles of His kingdom. I hope my story, and the lessons I've learned along the way, will bless you and inspire you to seek a more intimate walk with God as I've learned to enjoy.

For this reason I bow my knees to the Father of our Lord Jesus Christ, from whom the whole family in heaven and earth is named, that He would grant you, according to the riches of His glory, to be strengthened with might through His Spirit in the inner man, that Christ may dwell in your hearts through faith; that you, being rooted and grounded in love, may be able to comprehend with all the saints what is the width and length and depth and height—to know the love of Christ which passes knowledge; that you may be filled with all the fullness of God. Ephesians 3:14-19

This book contains the story of how God answered this prayer in my life.

1

An Unexpected Turn in the Road

You will keep him in perfect peace, whose mind is stayed on You, because he trusts in You. Isaiah 26:3

I watched anxiously from the bedroom window as the ambulance sped toward our house and into the driveway; then I ran downstairs to let the paramedics in. I was keenly aware that our nice, easy life would be different for a while. However, I had no idea that my own personal life was about to change – forever.

A half hour earlier my husband and I had settled ourselves for our usual Saturday evening routine in front of the TV when the phone rang. Upon hearing it was my sister calling from California, Alan knew I would be talking for a while, and since he wasn't feeling very well, he headed upstairs to lie down. Earlier that week an angiogram had shown he needed bypass surgery and an aortic valve replacement, and we had an appointment to meet with a surgeon the following Wednesday to make the arrangements. A few minutes into our sisterly chat, Alan broke in on our call. "Judy, I need you to come up here right away!" I hung up quickly and ran upstairs to discover my husband was having chest pains, an entirely new symptom. We prayed together, then I dialed 9-1-1.

Our local hospital ER doctor quickly determined they didn't have the facilities to provide the care Alan needed, so a helicopter was ordered to transport him to a larger hospital forty-five miles away. An hour later I arrived at the hospital to find him comfortably situated in a room. His condition had been stabilized and he was in good spirits. Surgery would take place on Monday or Tuesday. Though we didn't realize it, this was the beginning of our last ten weeks together. It was also the beginning of my closer, deeper walk with God in which I would discover the peace, joy, and strength that come through an intimate relationship with Him.

Just two weeks earlier on New Year's Day, I had chosen Isaiah 26:3 as my verse for the year: *You will keep him in perfect peace, whose mind is stayed on You, because he trusts in You.* My resolution was to learn how to stay my mind on God. Now Alan was in the hospital ICU, and I was facing problems completely beyond my ability to solve. In these unfamiliar and confusing surroundings, it was difficult to focus my thoughts on God at all, let alone stay them there.

Life on a Bench

The hospital room had a comfortable sleeping bench with storage drawers underneath. Since we lived so far from the hospital, Alan and I decided that I should stay in the room with him. I set up a little "campsite" in and around that bench, making myself as much at home as possible. It was not easy to get a good night's sleep with all the beeping monitors and nurses coming in and out, but I was close to Alan, and it was temporary. The doctor said we would be there for about three weeks. I found places for my clothes and other belongings and placed personal items around the room to make it feel more homelike for both of us.

The room had a bathroom with a shower. My first night there the nurse told me I was free to use the shower. Fortunately, before I did, another patient's wife warned me about the short shower curtain hanging beyond the edge of the shower that allowed water to run all over the bathroom floor. Before each shower I would need to track down the linen cart and obtain a large pile of towels for the purpose of mopping up afterward. There was no lock on the door (for patient safety, they said), so there was no guarantee that a staff person would not walk in on me. I put a note on the door before going in and tried to time my showers for when the nurse would be occupied elsewhere. Even so, the door was opened once just as I was stepping out. Fortunately, it was a female nurse! The toilet was for patient care, so I had to go down the hall and wait my turn at the public restroom. Since there was no lock on the door this was a good idea anyway.

My son and daughter heard about a nearby Family House where I could stay at a reasonable cost. It even had a shuttle to bring family members to and from the hospital. They suggested I look into it. I did, but I couldn't imagine being able to sleep very well away from Alan. The bench would have to be my home for the time being.

Surgery took place on Tuesday and was a success – six bypasses and a new valve. However, because Alan had been very weak prior to the operation, recovery would be slow. Yet, the doctors assured us we could expect a complete recovery. During the next three weeks, progress was slow but fairly steady. Getting him up to walk was a major production, but the physical therapist finally found the right piece of equipment, and Alan took several successful walks up and down the hall. He was also able to sit up for periods of time. Soon the doctor removed his feeding tube and said he could start eating regular food again. We were moving forward! After three and a half weeks it seemed as though the worst was over.

Exiled

Then suddenly it all turned upside down. After a very successful day where Alan took two good walks and stood up and brushed his teeth with help from the occupational therapist, we thought he was really on the road to recovery. The next morning, though, while working with the occupational therapist again, he began to shiver and had to sit under a pile of covers. The shivering finally stopped, and he ate a little lunch. Later that afternoon, one of our pastors and his wife stopped in to see us, and we all had a nice visit. Afterward, Alan and I talked for a few minutes. Little did we know this would be our last conversation together – ever. As we were talking, he began to shiver again. When that bout of shivering stopped, he sat back in the chair and said he felt better but needed to rest, so I went to my bench while he napped.

Around 6:00 p.m. the nurse asked if he was hungry. He said he would rather go to bed. She promised to come back soon and help him move from the chair to his bed. I began organizing food for my own dinner on an extra table and was getting ready to eat when the nurse returned. "So, Alan, are you ready to go to bed now?" No response. After a second attempt to get him to respond, she called for the charge nurse who ran in, grabbed Alan's feet, and lifted them into the air while telling the nurse, "Get him onto that bed right now!" The room immediately filled with medical personnel and equipment. I grabbed my dinner and left the room. Later I learned this was a code blue alert, but at the time I had no idea what was happening, except that it was obviously bad. I headed for the vestibule near the room and started sending urgent e-mails and texts requesting prayer.

The lady who stayed nights with the patient in the room next door saw all the commotion and came out to sit with me. She and I had become friends after three weeks of hospital dwelling. She calmed me down, and we prayed together. We tried to find out what was going on, but no one would talk to us. We peeked through an opening in the drawn curtains, but all we could see were people in blue and white uniforms surrounding the bed and lots of unfamiliar equipment. It was as if we didn't exist.

An hour or so later, I was allowed into the room briefly to get my purse and several other items. Upon entering, I noticed that my books and all the objects I had set around the room to make it look homey had been strewn every which way, and the bench was piled high with hospital equipment. At that moment the realization struck: that bench in the hospital room was not mine. My belongings were an intrusion into the business of getting people well. As long as the space wasn't needed for patient care, I was welcome to use it, but it didn't belong to me.

Before leaving the room, I told Alan that people all over the world were praying for him. I said the doctors wouldn't let me stay in the room, but I would be nearby. I returned to the vestibule. The doctor hurried past, saying, "I can't tell you anything right now."

The lady from next door advised me to try to sleep, so I tried. Feeling like an alien in a surreal land, I plugged my earbuds into my phone, turned on some praise music, curled up on the couch, and covered my head with my jacket. Around midnight the doctor tapped me on the shoulder. I sat up, instantly alert. He explained that Alan had experienced a "major septic episode." An infection somewhere in his body had wormed its way into the bloodstream making him "very, very sick." He had a high fever; his blood pressure had dropped to an alarming level, and there were many other frightening symptoms. The primary concern was that his kidneys were not working. If by 6:00 a.m. they didn't begin producing urine, dialysis would be a very real possibility. The doctor kept saying, "I'm so very sorry." Was he expecting Alan to die?

Throughout the night I dozed a little and prayed a lot. Many others were praying too. Amazingly, at 5:00 a.m. Alan's kidneys started working again! Later that morning my son, Doug, daughter, Julie, and her husband, Scott, drove from their homes two hundred miles away in suburban Chicago, arriving just as Alan went into surgery again. The doctors explored the colon area, expecting to locate the source of the infection. Nothing was found.

On My Own

During those first three and a half weeks in the hospital, I saw God's hand at work many times. The restarting of Alan's kidneys was truly a miracle. Miracles and answers to prayer were nothing new to us. In fact, Alan and I had walked with God for forty years, and we had seen Him do many amazing things. We had usually faced our trials together, but now Alan couldn't help me. He was unable to talk because the breathing tube had been reinserted. I could talk to him but would have to rely on those expressive eyes of his to read what he was saying back to me.

Even after my eviction from the bench, I still wanted to stay at the hospital, close to Alan, but my daughter and son-in-law finally convinced me to stay at their hotel for a night of beep-free sleep. Alan was sedated and wouldn't miss me. The next night he was still sedated, so I stayed at the hotel again. Without my realizing it at the time, my exile from that hospital room was to become a major turning point for me. After years of relying on Alan for many things, I would have to rely on God alone.

When I awoke after the second night at the hotel, I prayed for wisdom for the day, and two very clear thoughts came to me that I believe were from God. First, I would have Julie and

Scott help me move into the Family House before they left for home. A room in the Family House would be more conducive to sleep than the noisy hospital room, but the real issue was privacy and a safe place to keep my belongings. Since Alan would obviously be in the hospital for an extended period of time, I needed more than a bench behind a curtain. Second, I would ask Scott to help me buy a laptop computer and set it up so I wouldn't have to send e-mails from my phone, and I would not be limited to the sluggish, unreliable, and not-so-private computers in the hospital for taking care of banking and other matters that needed my attention.

When I called the Family House, the lady informed me that all the rooms were currently occupied. I was sure God had told me this was the time to move, so I asked her to call me when a room became available. As soon as I got off the phone, another patient's son told me he overheard my conversation, and he said his mother would be checking out of her room later that morning. I called the lady at Family House with this information, and my room was reserved. This was just one of many small miracles of God's perfect timing that continually encouraged me. Then at Walmart the exact computer I had in mind just happened to be on sale – another reason to praise God. We took it back to the hospital, and Scott made sure it was up and running. After helping me move my possessions to the Family House, Julie and Scott headed for home.

The next six weeks of my journey with Alan felt more like a roller coaster ride than a road trip. Going through all the details and ups and downs would serve no purpose in this book. This is not the story of Alan's illness and death but the story of my life as I went through that difficult period – and the exciting adventure with God I've been on ever since. For fifty-one years Alan was the driver and I was the passenger. Once we became Christians, God was the navigator. Sometimes we let Him sit in the front seat; occasionally we even let Him take the wheel. Until the very last couple of days, I expected that eventually Alan and I would return home to keep traveling through life together; instead, he went on the ultimate journey to be with his Lord and Savior, and I continued the earthly journey as a "singled-out" woman.

During those days in the Family House, I began to discover the joy and peace that come when we let God be the planner, the navigator, *and* the driver. In this time of utter helplessness, I found new strength. It took a while for me to recognize it and learn to walk it out, but a transformation was taking place in me as I learned how to draw on the mighty power of the Holy Spirit.

Obviously when I moved to the Family House, I had no idea God might be preparing me to travel through life without Alan, but there was a sense of newness about my life from the moment I said goodbye to the kids and shut the door. Away from the chaos of the hospital, I knew I could center my thoughts on God. There I would learn how to stay my thoughts on Him and find perfect peace. Although Alan and I would still be traveling together for a few more weeks, God was gently preparing me for the rocky road ahead and for the adventures to follow with Him in the driver's seat.

2

Spiritual Photosynthesis

*Blessed is the man who walks not in the counsel of
the ungodly, nor stands in the path of sinners, nor
sits in the seat of the scornful; but his delight is in
the law of the LORD, and in His law he meditates
day and night. He shall be like a tree planted by the
rivers of water, that brings forth its fruit in its sea-
son, whose leaf also shall not wither; and whatever
he does shall prosper.* Psalm 1:1-3

This psalm has been a favorite of mine for years. I always
wanted to be like the man in this vivid description –
planted, established firmly, bringing forth fruit, flourishing,
and prospering. He is the very picture of strength. The passage
makes it very clear what we must do to be like him. Three things
we must avoid: walking in ungodly counsel, standing with sinners, and sitting in the seat of the scornful. Two things we must
do instead: delight in God's Word and keep it continually in
our thoughts. For years I believed I was doing all of this, yet I
bore little resemblance to the man in the psalm. The strength
we see here is available to all believers. God has provided it for

all of us by grace – undeserved favor, not based on our own merit. Yet, to experience it in our lives, we must each access it by faith. It does not come automatically.

We can gain insight into the process of spiritual growth by considering the life processes in a tree. To grow and bear fruit, a tree must first of all have nutrients. These minerals and other substances are in the soil. The tree also needs water, which brings nutrients up from the soil through the roots and trunk and into the leaves. Without the action of water to carry these materials, they would remain in the ground completely useless to the tree. Sunlight aids in upward movement of water by pulling it out of the leaves through evaporation, which brings nutrients to the leaves. Then it enables a complex chemical reaction that nurtures the tree and keeps it alive. With proper amounts of nutrients, water, and sunlight, the tree will thrive and be productive.

The necessary elements for a healthy, fruitful spiritual life in a believer are similar to the physical needs of a tree. The nutrients, of course, are knowledge, wisdom, and understanding, which we gain through reading, studying, and meditating on God's Word. King Solomon told his son, *seek her* [understanding] *as silver, and search for her as for hidden treasures,* and *the* LORD *gives wisdom; from His mouth come knowledge and understanding* (Proverbs 2:4, 6). In the New Testament, the apostle Paul advised Timothy, *Be diligent to present yourself approved to God, a worker who does not need to be ashamed, rightly dividing the word of truth* (2 Timothy 2:15). He instructed the church in Rome, *Do not be conformed to this world, but be transformed by the renewing of your mind* (Romans 12:2). This renewing is accomplished through learning and understanding the Word.

Just as a farmer may enrich the soil around his trees with fertilizer, we can speed up our spiritual progress by reading Christian books and listening to others who have already invested time and effort in this endeavor. God has placed teachers in the body of Christ to help us understand the Bible. However, to develop our full potential, we must read and study it for ourselves. Learning God's Word is like putting down roots into the soil to draw out precious nutrients buried there just for us. The farmer can fertilize the soil, but the tree has to dig in! Spiritual growth requires mental effort on our part.

Alan and I were not lacking in this area. We gave our lives to Jesus in 1972, and by the time we arrived at the hospital, we had forty years of church attendance and Bible study under our belts. We diligently read God's Word and endeavored to live by it. Recently we had even spent two years taking online Bible college courses. We were well versed on what the Bible had to say about most subjects. Unfortunately, much of what we had learned and studied never made it from our minds to our hearts, and that was the problem.

No matter how rich the soil may be, water must transport the nutrients to where the tree can use them. Likewise, no matter how much we expose ourselves to God's Word, it must be carried to our hearts before we can use it. We bring biblical truths into our minds, but revelation from the Holy Spirit must flow from our mind to our heart where we can apply it to our lives. Have you ever experienced an Aha! moment when a familiar passage of Scripture suddenly becomes alive for you with new, personal meaning? This is an example of the work of the Holy Spirit, revealing the Word to your heart.

When praying for the Ephesian church, the apostle Paul asked God to give the believers *the spirit of wisdom and revelation in the knowledge of Him* that they might know who they are in Christ and what they have access to through Him (Ephesians 1:15:20). It is not enough to have knowledge; we also need wisdom and revelation from the Holy Spirit. Yet, this does not minimize the importance of knowledge. The wisdom and revelation Paul spoke of are *in the knowledge* of Him. If we haven't put knowledge into our mind, the Holy Spirit can't reveal anything to us about it.

In my forty years as a Christian, I experienced many moments of wisdom and revelation. I remember one summer when Alan and I were looking for a new home. We had begun the delightful practice of taking a nap every afternoon. We would lie down, and almost immediately Alan would be sound asleep. Not being a day sleeper, I would use the time to close my eyes and meditate on passages of Scripture. Several times the Holy Spirit revealed exciting connections between various passages and showed me how they applied to my current situation. I really enjoyed these insights, but once we began packing and moving, we became too busy for naps. Because these times with God had not become a priority, I let them get lost in the shuffle. I had the nutrients of the Word and the living water of the Holy Spirit, but I was lacking a vital element.

The Importance of Sunlight

We know a tree needs sunlight in order to survive, but many people don't understand why. Sunlight plays such a vital role that the life-giving process of making food for the tree is called *photosynthesis. Photo* is the Greek word for light. Photosynthesis takes place in the leaf. In this process, carbon dioxide from the air combines chemically with water from within the leaf to give off oxygen and form a sugar called glucose, which then incorporates other nutrients to feed the tree. Energy from the sun becomes trapped in the sugar molecules. As the tree grows, further chemical reaction releases the energy stored in the sugar molecules, using it to fuel all of the tree's other life processes, including production of fruit.

In our spiritual growth, God's presence operates much like the sunlight in photosynthesis. In a tree, all the action takes place in the leaves. In us, the action of the Holy Spirit takes place in our hearts. Our quiet time alone with God allows the nutrient-rich Word that comes into our hearts to combine with refreshing revelation from the Holy Spirit. In the same way that a tree traps sugar molecules in the leaves, we capture and release spiritual energy in our hearts by basking in the presence of God.

A farmer's primary interest in a fruit tree is in the fruit it produces. He takes care of the tree so it will bear fruit. So it is with God and us. He wants our lives to be fruitful and productive. He has given us His Word to nourish and renew our minds, the Holy Spirit to reveal truths from His Word to our hearts, and the light of His presence to energize and sustain us. If we neglect any of these three components, our growth will be stunted, and our fruit will be less than what God wants for us.

Such was the state I was in when Alan and I arrived at the hospital. I had knowledge of the Bible, and the Holy Spirit had revealed connections to me. But because I didn't spend regular time in the presence of God, I was like a tree digging roots into nutrient-rich soil but not getting enough sunlight to draw the water upward. Instead of flourishing vigorously, my leaves were withering. The little fruit I was able to produce fell far short of what God wanted for me. When I came up against a problem – from a cranky stepmother's demands to a computer malfunction – instead of manifesting love, joy, peace, and patience, I had the tendency to fall apart as if God had gone out of town that day.

God promises that if we seek Him, we will find Him – if we seek with our whole heart (Jeremiah 29:13). He had been patiently waiting for me to do this. He was ready for me all along, but I had to make the decision. Now my desire for a closer walk with Him was serious; and as I began seeking Him, He not only allowed me, but helped me, to find Him. After forty years of strolling casually with God, I was about to embark upon a purposeful, intimate walk with Him through heights and depths I could never have imagined.

A Better Environment

When Alan and I were uprooted from our quiet, comfortable home and transplanted to a room in the noisy, busy ICU, I found my New Year's resolution – to keep my mind stayed on God – severely challenged. I might find a place of quiet retreat one day, only to have it intruded upon the next day. In that environment, opportunities for private moments of quiet reflection were few and far between. After more than three weeks surrounded by chaos, the peaceful quiet of the Family House would give me a place where I could have those moments of quiet reflection. During the next few weeks, I would become increasingly aware of God's presence. He would continually encourage me, sustain me, and surprise me with unexpected blessings and answers to prayer.

My new dwelling place was nothing fancy, but to me it was pure luxury: a clean, quiet, second-floor room with a private bathroom and a door with a secure lock. I could take a leisurely bath or shower without worrying that someone might walk in. Instead of a bench and a windowsill, I had comfortable twin beds and a closet and dresser for my clothes. I had a nice easy chair by the window, a truly high-speed internet connection, and my own TV. My belongings and I were secure.

Downstairs, beyond the hotel-like lobby, a large shared kitchen served as a gathering place for the residents. I quickly became acquainted with other long-term guests. Only a person who has been through a similar situation can understand the importance of these short-term relationships with other people who are going through similar battles. Usually when I returned there for the evening, I would have a snack and visit for a few minutes, but it would not be long before I escaped to the peace and privacy of my own room.

The first morning there I got out of bed, put on my clothes, went down to the kitchen for a large cup of coffee, and brought it up to my room. I settled into the comfy chair. A few days earlier at the hospital, the lady next door had given me a small devotional book entitled *Jesus Calling* by Sarah Young. I had read the introduction and leafed through the book at the hospital. It sounded interesting, but I had not started reading it. That morning it occurred to me that since God put it on my friend's heart to give me the book, He probably wanted me to read it!

After a brief prayer lifting up the day, I opened the book to that day's entry. The message began, "Peace be with you," and talked about the price Jesus paid on the cross for our peace. It encouraged the reader to sit quietly in His presence and experience His peace – just what I needed to hear and to do. I sat there quietly for a few minutes as I finished my coffee. Then off I went to wait for the shuttle to the hospital.

The next day I started again with coffee, prayer, and *Jesus Calling*. This entry encouraged me not to give in to fear and worry but to fix my eyes on Jesus. It was as if the book had been written just for me. After reading the message, I pondered it quietly before going off to face whatever the day might hold for me. I continued to begin each day the same way. God spoke to me in amazing ways through that book. Each day's entry seemed to target exactly the concerns I had for that day, and resting and reflecting on the devotional helped center me.

I wish I could say that from that first day at the Family House, I faced each day unafraid and brimming over with peace and joy. Most days I did start out that way, but the circumstances around me would gradually pull my thoughts away from God and His goodness. I would find myself focusing on what was happening in the hospital room. This was, of course, a perfectly natural response to what was going on around me, but it was not beneficial to my spiritual growth. Even so, despite my inability to remain steadfast in my thinking, God remained steadfast. He knew my heart's desire to walk more closely with Him.

The next few days we were full of hope as Alan began to perk up and respond to us. Each day brought some improvement. The miraculous restarting of his kidneys after the septic episode had begun a period of recovery. Meanwhile, the doctors continued to look for the source and site of infection and attempted to fight off whatever had caused it. As Alan progressed, he participated in prayers and Bible reading by squeezing my hand or even raising his hands a little as I said "Amen." The doctors said they were very encouraged at his progress.

Another Turn for the Worse

Then after five days of steady improvement, Alan had another septic episode, which left him much weaker than before. Now the level of creatinine in his blood (an indication of kidney function) and white blood cell count (an indication of infection in the bloodstream) became major issues. The doctors still believed a full recovery was possible, but they needed to identify the infection in order to fight it effectively. They never did. They did all that was medically possible to hunt down and destroy that elusive enemy, but it remained a mystery to the last day.

To be like the fruitful tree, we must delight ourselves in the law of the Lord (His Word) and meditate on it day and night. Instead, much of the time I found myself meditating on pulses, respiration numbers, and levels of creatinine and white blood cells – things I had absolutely no control over. For me, this was a form of *walking in the counsel of the ungodly*. Medical personnel were not ungodly in the sense of being evil, but their counsel was based only on what could be perceived by the five senses or by their sophisticated equipment.

Whereas it was the responsibility of the doctors and nurses to monitor these physical facts, it would have been more productive for me to keep my own thoughts focused on spiritual truths. Instead, my thinking tended to wander back and forth between the two. When Alan was awake and no one was working on him, I read the Bible to him, prayed, sang Scripture songs, talked about the kids and grandkids, and played praise music. But when a nurse, doctor, or therapist came in, I sat aside on the bench watching, listening, and grasping for any tidbit of good news. All of the truly good news I'd just been reading, talking, and singing about was forgotten – or took a back seat to the words of the professionals.

I'm sure if I had been able to focus on the goodness of God instead of the circumstances, I would have experienced more peace, as promised in my New Year scripture. Whether this would have affected the outcome for Alan in any way, no one will ever know. It certainly wouldn't have done him any harm, and it would have been very good for me. With the perspective of hindsight, I can see all of this; but at the time, things were happening faster than I could process them, and there's no point in condemning myself now for things I didn't do then.

Learning to Listen

After a few weeks at the Family House, I decided to take advantage of this quiet, private place to spend more time alone with God. I woke up as usual, put on my clothes, got my coffee, and settled into the chair. Then I looked at my watch: 6:30 a.m. I thanked God for the day. I told Him, "This next half hour is Yours. I know the whole day is Yours, and I should be listening to You all day, and I will try; but for sure this next thirty minutes I'll stay right here listening for Your voice. I'll spend part of the time in Your Word. If there's something You want to show me, I'm ready. Otherwise, I'll just wait."

I read the daily devotional, then sat quietly. I looked at my watch: 6:37. Hmmm. I sat quietly. 6:42. Hmmm. I read a couple chapters, probably in Romans or Ephesians. 6:47. That half hour seemed very long. When I got up from the chair, I did feel much calmer than I had felt the last few weeks. No messages, no lightning bolts, no overwhelming sense of God's presence; but I knew I had been with Him.

The next morning I prayed, "Lord, Your Word says You are my Shepherd. You say that Your sheep hear Your voice. You don't say we might hear it or that we should try to hear it, but that we do. I know You are always talking to me. Please help me be more sensitive to Your voice." I continued to start each day with thirty minutes of listening for God's voice, beginning with the devotional. Some mornings I felt His tangible presence; other days I felt nothing. Sometimes I talked to Him; other times I was very quiet. Occasionally a passage of Scripture would come to mind, and I would look it up and meditate on it. Every day was different.

My relationship with God gradually changed. The first day of my thirty-minute commitment, I sat obediently in the chair, not knowing what to expect. Just the act of quieting my heart for thirty minutes required effort. After a couple weeks, though, I was hurrying to dress, get my coffee, and settle into my chair. No longer just an act of obedience, this half hour had become a precious part of my day. A few times the coffee sat neglected, as I just relaxed and enjoyed the awareness of God's presence. Other days I had to struggle to stay focused.

Whether or not the time felt productive on any particular day, I treasured that half hour alone with God before going out into a world riddled with ups and downs. I was spending time in the sunlight of God's presence, and spiritual photosynthesis was beginning to take place, preparing my heart and strengthening me for what was to come in the days ahead.

3

Losing the Fear — Finding the Power

*There is no fear in love; but perfect love casts out
fear, because fear involves torment. But he who fears
has not been made perfect in love.* 1 John 4:18

The journal I kept and emails I sent while Alan was in the
hospital paint a clear picture of events during the ten-week
period. They also show my emotions and attitudes. Most impor-
tantly, they chronicle my journey into a more consistent trust
in God and His love. As we dealt with all the ups and downs
in Alan's situation, circumstances were rocky even on the best
days. Yet, God was graciously revealing more and more of His
amazing love and grace toward me as the days passed.

Throughout most of my adult life I was plagued by fear,
mainly because I had an unclear understanding of who God
really is. I knew He loved me – He had to, in order to remain
true to His Word, right? But I wasn't sure He liked me. I didn't
feel secure in His love. Many of His promises seemed condi-
tional on my doing things right. I always felt as if I fell short of
my dad's expectations of me and then my husband's, so when I

became a Christian, I carried those same feelings of inadequacy into my relationship with God.

In more recent years, I began to understand that righteousness was a gift, not something I had to earn. While I found this truth very comforting, there was still something lacking. I didn't *feel* God's love. When I first asked Jesus into my heart, I felt His love and peace washing over me. The warm glow lasted for several weeks before gradually fading. I always hoped to feel that way again, but even after I had moved past thinking I had to do everything right in order to gain God's approval, I still was not able to reach the depth of peace and contentment I experienced at the beginning.

Now during my times with God at the Family House, I began having genuine love encounters with Him. These were delightful moments. Inevitably the hospital beckoned because I really wanted to be with Alan. Even so, the daily commitment to spend time with God every morning was changing me. I was opening my heart and allowing the Holy Spirit to work, and He was building the strength I would need in the weeks and months ahead. Gradually, without my conscious awareness, fear was being replaced with strength. *For God has not given us a spirit of fear, but of power and of love and of a sound mind* (2 Timothy 1:7).

Conquering Fear of Driving

One major area of fear had to do with driving. Although at one time I fearlessly drove vanloads of high school kids with various behavioral and emotional problems to and from school every day, eventually my career changed, and my job no longer involved driving. In fact, for the last fifteen years before retiring, I didn't even drive to and from work. I rode the commuter train. After I retired, except for an occasional jaunt to the grocery store or the mall, I had little occasion to drive. I left that responsibility in Alan's capable hands. He enjoyed driving; I was happy to be a passenger. Somehow during that time I gradually lost confidence in my ability to drive, and I avoided getting behind the wheel unless absolutely necessary.

A few days after Alan was admitted to the hospital, my son took me home to get the car and bring it to the hospital. Nervous or not, I would need to drive. Intimidated by the parking garage, I was thankful for the free valet parking service. With trepidation I ventured forth to nearby grocery stores and ran other necessary errands. I also had to make the forty-five-mile trip home every once in a while. Hospital or no hospital, mail kept coming, bills needed to be paid, and the responsibility involved in caring for my ninety-four-year-old stepmother (in a nursing home) didn't stop just because I wasn't living at home.

Added to my general discomfort with driving around in an unfamiliar city, I couldn't call Alan to help me if I encountered any sort of problem. And my kids were two hundred miles away. Because car care had been so remote from my thinking for so many years, it never occurred to me to glance at the gas gauge until, when returning from my second trip home, I felt the car slowing to a stop on the interstate. Oops! Out of gas. Fortunately, I was near an exit, and my fear didn't extend to using my cell phone. A highway patrolman soon came to rescue me, and he was very kind and non-judgmental.

Eventually, I became more confident about driving. I learned to navigate the parking garage and stopped using the shuttle to get to and from the Family House. Driving my own car gave me more time to spend with Alan and allowed me to make sure he was properly tucked in for the night before I left. I even started giving rides back and forth to other Family House residents.

I was doing fine with driving until the morning I walked out of the Family House to discover a windshield covered with sticky seed pods brought down by rain during the night. I turned on the wipers, which only created a gooey mess. I had no idea how to operate the windshield washer because I never had an occasion to use it. The owner's manual was no help; I did what I thought it said but obviously didn't understand the instructions. In a hurry to get to the hospital, I headed on down the street, peering through streaks and praying for angelic protection, knowing I would need to solve this problem before making the return trip that night in the dark.

I couldn't think of anyone to call, so I prayed, "Lord, thank You that You will show me someone to ask about this today." As I approached the parking garage, a car exactly like mine entered the line a few spaces ahead of me. Pulling into my usual slot, I noticed that the other car had pulled in facing me on the other side of the dividing wall. I expected the driver to walk toward the hospital entrance, but instead, he walked in the opposite direction, around the wall, and right toward my car. I rolled down my window as he came near and asked if he would show me how to run the windshield washer. One little pull in the right direction, using the right handle, and out came the washer fluid. Nothing to it when you know how!

All that morning I rejoiced over God's perfect, simple answer to my prayer. How awesome that the Creator of the universe had intervened in my life, showing me His love and care in a tangible way. I'm glad the owner's manual didn't make sense because I needed a touch from God that day more than a clean windshield, and I ended up with both. Daily interactions and interventions like this reassured me that whatever was happening with Alan, God was watching over me. The deep, sure conviction of God's presence was growing in my life and heart. I was beginning to feel His love.

Attitude Adjustment

Thankfulness was an important key to my spiritual growth at

that time. Although my journal is full of little medical details, it is also filled with expressions of thankfulness to the Lord for perfect timing, for the people He put around me to help, and for wisdom and insight. As I wrote the daily e-mails, I made it a point to find reasons to thank and praise God. Some days the circumstances were negative, but when there was no good news to share, I would give thanks for a scripture that was blessing me or a song that was going through my mind. We can't conjure up feelings of joy, but we can always choose to be thankful, and thankfulness brings joy.

Gratitude for God's goodness brought joy that made no sense in the natural realm. It is obvious from reading my journal, although I was not aware of it, the end was drawing near for Alan. Every forward step was followed by two steps backward. Immersed in the details each day, I didn't see the big picture. Of course I had panicky moments, times of discouragement, and feelings of loss and sadness. Even though Alan was there in the room with me, he wasn't really there, and I never knew for sure what he was thinking. I knew he wanted me to "fix it" so we could go back home, and I was frustrated that I couldn't. Yet, underneath all of these unpleasant emotions, I felt an undercurrent of joy. God's Word tells us, *The joy of the Lord is your strength* (Nehemiah 8:10). In direct contrast to what was happening around me, strength was emerging within me. This was not my own natural joy and strength; it was truly supernatural.

On February 3, a week before the first septic episode, I wrote in my journal:

> *I've just realized that I have been depending on Alan*
> *for a lot of things. Some were realistic: putting gas*
> *in the car, for example. Others were not fair: how I*
> *felt about myself, approval, or emotional support.*
> *For these things I should have been trusting in the*
> *Lord. My self-image should have been based on how*

God sees me. I should have been resting in His love.
Instead, I looked to Alan. I relied on his strength
instead of on God's. I need to focus on my relation-
ship with God, not other people.

I realized it was a mistake to look to other people, even our spouses, for approval and assurance of our self-worth. Our emotional well-being suffers when we use other people as our mirror, and it puts an unfair burden on them as well. God wants us to use His Word as our mirror. There we learn how He sees us; we find we are *accepted in the Beloved* (Ephesians 1:6). Learning to rely on Jesus to meet our emotional needs frees us from dependence on others, enabling us to become better spouses, parents, and friends.

I also wrote about needing to get my focus off the physical realm and keep my mind "stayed on God," referring to my New Year's resolution. Many Bible passages tell us to do this. Romans 8:5 really nails the point: *For those who live according to the flesh set their minds on the things of the flesh, but those who live according to the Spirit, the things of the Spirit.* I had thought I was living according to the Spirit, but when life threw me a curve, I became acutely aware of just where I was on the "Flesh/Spirit Scale." Because I hadn't made time with God a priority, I was double minded. I didn't have the mental steadfastness and emotional stability that comes from intimacy with God.

Putting It in God's Hands

Although we were not able to overcome Alan's illness, my daily times in the presence of God were having an effect on my heart. As Alan's physical condition grew weaker, my relationship with God continued to grow stronger. Every day I saw evidence of His love and care. In Isaiah 30:15 God says, *In returning and rest you shall be saved; in quietness and confidence shall be your strength.* My confidence in God was growing despite the negative circumstances, and I was finding strength. Then a week or so before Alan's death, sitting on my bed in the Family House at the end of a particularly difficult day, I completely surrendered the whole situation to God. I was praying according to Philippians 4:6-7, *Be anxious for nothing, but in everything by prayer and supplication, with thanksgiving, let your requests be made known to God; and the peace of God, which surpasses all understanding, will guard your hearts and minds through Christ Jesus.*

"Father," I said, "I choose right now to be anxious for nothing, *nothing*. As I see it, there are three possible ways this can go: Alan could walk out of the hospital totally and miraculously healed (this is obviously my first request); he could leave recovering, needing lots of help and support from me to see him through all the therapy (that would be my second request); or he could die. Of course I don't want him to die. I want him to receive his healing and come home. But Your Word promises that Your peace, which passes all understanding, will guard *my* heart and mind in Christ Jesus, regardless of how things turn out. So Lord, I put this in Your hands. Whatever the outcome, I want You to know I will not be afraid. I know You love me, and I will trust You."

Believe it or not, this was the first time it dawned on me that Alan might not be coming home with me. But even with that realization, I slept peacefully that night, secure in the knowledge that however things might go with Alan, I would be okay. This was definitely the promised *peace that passes all understanding.*

Singled Out

A few days later, a nurse practitioner came into Alan's room and asked me to stay close by. The doctor would be there soon and wanted to talk with me. I knew there had been a serious septic episode around midnight and things were rapidly deteriorating. Now the doctor wanted to talk to me. It was clear that we were in trouble. It was midafternoon. Alan was sleeping, and I was sitting on my bench waiting for the doctor, when Pastor Paul from our church walked in. When I told him what was going on, he said, "Well, then, I guess I'm here for you this time, not for Alan."

He told me he had actually been planning to visit the next day but had received a strong impression that God wanted him to come today. Then when he got into his car to make the forty-five-mile trip, it occurred to him that it was his wife's lunch hour, and he could go for a walk with her before heading toward the hospital. So, he spent that hour with her before driving over. The perfect timing of Pastor Paul's visit was powerful evidence to me that God was watching over me. Had he not obeyed those promptings of the Holy Spirit, I would have been alone when the doctor came to talk with me.

We had just finished reading Romans 8 and praying when the nurse practitioner came back. He said the doctor had been called away, so he would talk to us instead. We moved to an adjoining room, where he explained that they had done all they could for Alan. The twenty or so pumps of medicine were keeping him alive, but it was no longer a matter of maintaining him till his body started to kick in and recover. Now they were just postponing the inevitable because his kidneys were no longer functioning. The doctor recommended stopping the medications. I chose to wait till the next day when Julie could be there with me.

Pastor Paul and I went back into Alan's room. Now Alan was awake. I told him we had just been talking with the doctor, and it looked as if it might be time for him to go home and be with the Lord. He looked worried. I think he was worried about what would happen to me without him. I wondered the same thing. Even in our pre-Christian, not-so-happily-married days, Alan had always been very solicitous about my welfare.

Pastor Paul told me it was very important to reassure Alan that I would be okay, so I did. I told him God had been taking awesome care of me while he was in the hospital, and so had the kids. I told him I was no longer nervous about driving, had all of our financial matters under control, and would sell the house and move to an easy-care condo near the kids. He looked less worried and more relaxed after that. I said I was still praying and believing for a miraculous healing, but if we didn't see it this side of heaven, and he had to leave, I would not be worried about him. Although I wouldn't know what he was doing, I would always know where he was; by the time I arrived to join him, he would know where everything was and could show me around. Hearing those words, his facial expression seemed to brighten.

The next day Julie arrived. Doug couldn't be there, but from home he was able to spare me the agonizing task of making arrangements with the funeral home and cemetery, a job I had really been dreading. We talked with Alan, but he was in and out of consciousness as we tried to say our goodbyes. The medicines were stopped, and as predicted, his body shut down. Within a few short hours he was gone. He was free at last – free from sickness, weakness, and fear; free from worry and stress; free to enjoy God's presence forever. When I think of Alan in heaven, I picture him dancing and rejoicing with abandon.

Here on earth a chapter in my life had ended. The road was taking a new turn. I had been singled-out for a new journey with God. Just as I had declared a few nights earlier, I was not afraid. Given my choice, I would have opted for a different path, one with Alan still by my side. But I was ready for whatever God had for me. I would go through some rough patches along that new road, but fear would not be my unwelcome companion. God had given me *power, and love, and a sound mind* (2 Timothy 1:17).

4

Hearing God's Voice

The sheep hear his voice; and he calls his own sheep by name, and leads them out ... and the sheep follow him, for they know his voice. John 10:3-4

In previous chapters I've talked about listening for God's voice. Although God has never actually spoken to me in an audible voice, many times I've been absolutely sure what I heard was from Him. How do we hear His voice, and how do we distinguish it from all the other voices clamoring for our attention?

Jesus uses the intimate, loving relationship between a shepherd and his sheep to emphasize the importance of hearing His voice. Most of us in this modern culture have never seen a shepherd, but we are familiar with Psalm 23 where David depicts God's tender, watchful care for us. We know a shepherd has total care of the sheep and provides for their needs by leading them to the best grazing areas and the good drinking water. He watches over them and keeps them from harm, even going so far as to fight off enemy intruders.

This sheep-shepherd relationship is an excellent comparison to our relationship with God. In places where sheep are still raised on open land in a natural setting, a newborn lamb very quickly becomes attuned to the voice of its owner. A love relationship develops between them. The owner calls the sheep by name, and it comes to him. If someone else tries to call it, though he may use the same words and vocal inflections he has heard the shepherd use, the sheep will not respond. It will simply stand there looking at him as if to say, "Who are you?"

I remember hearing a visitor to Israel describe watching a group of three shepherds talking with one another in a field. As they conversed, their flocks gradually mingled into one big, unorganized group. Watching the sheep milling around, the visitor wondered how the owners would ever be able to sort out the sheep that belonged to them. But when it was time to leave, each shepherd began calling and gently talking to his sheep, and as the three men went their separate ways, each man's sheep followed him. They knew their masters' voices.

In John 10:1-16 (NASB) Jesus was trying to convey to His disciples the interaction God wants with His followers. He described a good shepherd; then He said, *The sheep hear his voice; and he calls his own sheep by name, and leads them out ... the sheep follow him because they know his voice. And a stranger they simply will not follow, but will flee from him, because they do not know the voice of strangers* (vv. 3-5). Although the disciples undoubtedly knew more than we do about the behavioral tendencies of sheep, the Bible tells us they didn't understand what Jesus was saying to them. So He continued the explanation by contrasting a shepherd with a thief, and told them plainly, *I am the good shepherd; and I know My own, and My own know Me* (v. 14).

Learning to Listen

God speaks to us in many ways. As our intimacy with Him deepens, we become better at hearing His voice. My morning times in the Family House served as a training ground for becoming more closely attuned to God. Am I saying that before then I never heard God's voice? Of course not. My walk with God was filled with amazing experiences where He spoke to me and gave me wisdom, guidance, and encouragement. One of the ministries of the Holy Spirit is to teach us and lead us into all truth (John 16:13). But I would characterize most of those earlier encounters as "believing and receiving." They were not based on intimacy.

God's mercy and grace are so overwhelming that He will answer our prayers and supply our needs even though we have not sought Him with our whole heart. Such a relationship, though, is based on what God can do for us, not on appreciating Him for who He is. The true desire for a deeper relationship with God fueled my Family House experience. There, for the first time in my life, I longed only to know Him better. I was not asking Him to do anything for me other than to reveal Himself more fully. The word *intimacy* didn't enter the conversation, but that was what I hungered for, and that was what developed.

The Living Word

As we grow closer to God, we develop a heightened awareness of His voice. Because He knows each of us by name (including our individual personalities), there is infinite variety in the ways He interacts with us. However, most of the ways God speaks to His children fall into three main categories: the written Word, the spoken word, and His still, small voice.

We should be expecting God to speak to us through His Word, but He can only do this if we are actually reading it. But how do you know where to read? Should you follow a schedule? Or should you just let the Bible fall open and assume whatever catches your eye is God's word for you today (sort of like a Christian Ouija board)? While it isn't necessary to follow a schedule, for me it helps to begin with some kind of plan. Otherwise, I will end up flipping through pages, not really reading or focusing on anything.

The most important plan is to sit down, open the Bible, and *read.* Sounds like a no-brainer, but many people never get to that step, or at least not very often. There are as many ways to approach reading the Bible as there are people reading it, but I will explain one method that works for me. If you don't already have a plan of your own, you might give it a try. The very loose plan I follow most days is reading through the New Testament at my own pace. One day I may read a chapter, another day several chapters, another day one or two verses. Occasionally I may camp on one verse or passage for several days.

Instead of reading all four Gospels (Matthew, Mark, Luke, and John) one after the other, I start by reading the gospel of Matthew, skipping the other three Gospels and reading straight through from the book of Acts to the end. The next time I start with Mark, skip over to Acts and on to the end. Each time I begin with a different gospel. As I follow this plan, when something interests me or grabs my attention, I stop there, pray about it, or look up the verse in a commentary. While I admit some days I find myself reading and getting nothing, it is absolutely amazing how often a passage or verse in the course of this daily reading will be exactly what I need that very day.

Recently, I was struggling with a lack of discipline or structure in my life, sometimes letting a whole day pass by without exercising, practicing my cello, or accomplishing anything really worthwhile. Deciding it was time to get a handle on the situation, I set up a daily routine including all the things I needed to do each day. I had a logical time and order for accomplishing each, making allowances for day-to-day fluctuations in my schedule. While I was at it, I also threw in a few guidelines to help myself eat right and restrict my TV watching. No surprise that by the third day of this wonderful, thoughtfully devised system, I was unable to follow the plan.

Feeling like a failure, I devised a daily checklist to track my accomplishments. Then I prayed over the checklist, asking God for more self-control and declaring it was mine by faith as a fruit of the Spirit. Do you see what was wrong with this picture? Well, I didn't! But a couple mornings later, following my regular Bible-reading plan, I came to Philippians 1:6 (NASB). *For I am confident of this very thing, that He who began a good work in you will perfect it until the day of Christ Jesus.* I felt like the guy in the TV ad who slaps his forehead and exclaims, "I could've had a V-8!"

"Oh, my goodness, Lord," I said. "I'm trying to do all this in my own flesh, by my own strength, instead of letting You work in me." Realizing how *self*-focused my system was, I let go of the schedule and the teeth-gritting, gonna-do-it-no-matter-what mentality. Peace and joy returned.

I would still like to become more diligent in these areas, but it will not happen by my efforts. The same God who put the desire in my heart to start cello lessons, and has shown me when and where to walk every day without making a big deal out of it, will provide the encouragement and reminders to do these things. He can also be trusted to show me what to eat and what to watch on TV. Instead of having more rules to follow, I need to be more sensitive to His leading each day. When God brings about changes in our lives, it is almost effortless on our part. We don't even realize they're taking place until we look back later and see the difference.

I love those times when a passage jumps out and says, "Here's your answer." The Philippians verse certainly was not new to me. I had even underlined it. But out of the whole Bible, that gentle correction was what I needed to hear that day. Sheep not only hear their shepherd's voice, they also follow it. I had to respond to what God had just shown me. Had I just said, "Wow, that is so cool," and then continued trying to straighten out my life under my own steam, the Word from God would have had no effect on me.

At other times, before I even open my Bible, an already familiar verse may come to mind. Jesus said the Holy Spirit would bring to our remembrance all He has said to us (John 14:26). When that happens, I put my reading plan on hold and go to that verse. The best part of my reading plan is that I don't have to complete a certain amount of reading within a given time period. My flesh loves to make rules, cleverly disguised as guidelines, turning what could be a precious time to interact with God into a religion. This plan with its deliberate lack of time frame avoids that. Sometimes I deviate from the plan altogether and spend a few days or weeks reading in the Old Testament where many spiritual nuggets are buried just waiting for me to dig them up. In the back of this book, you'll find books with other Bible-reading plans. The plan you choose is not the issue. The important thing is to interact with God daily through His Word.

He Knows Where I Am

Although the Bible has been around for thousands of years and has been read by millions of people, God still uses it to speak very intimately, individually, and specifically to each of us. A recent experience illustrates this very well. Alan's sister Ruth who lived in Alabama was also a new widow and invited me to join her on a trip to Alaska with her senior citizens group. After almost a year of talking and planning, the big day came for our trip-of-a-lifetime. As I put the final touches on my packing, the words came to mind, *You will go out in joy and be led forth in peace.* I knew it was a Bible verse, or part of one, but didn't know the exact reference.

Walking out the door, I heard the words again. "Thank You, Lord," I said. "I receive Your joy and peace." But that wasn't all He wanted to tell me. Feeling very joyful and peaceful I arrived at the airport, checked my bag, and had just cleared security when I received a call from the travel coordinator in Alabama telling me Ruth was too sick and weak to make the trip. Ruth had not been feeling well, but neither of us realized the extent of her illness. So there I was – the woman who less than two years before was apprehensive about driving two miles from the hospital to the Family House – fearlessly preparing to board an airplane to fly four *thousand* miles to spend two weeks with a group of total strangers.

At the gate as I awaited my flight, the phrase came to mind once again, so I looked it up on Google. The verse was Isaiah 55:12 (NIV). *You will go out in joy and be led forth in peace; the mountains and hills will burst forth into song before you, and all the trees of the field will clap their hands.* My heart jumped. Suddenly the verse became much more personal to me, since I was heading to a place known for its mountains and trees. It was as if God had just said, "I know where you're going, and I'll be right there with you." Although I was disappointed that I would not be sharing this experience with Ruth, joy and peace surrounded me like a cloud. I flew from Chicago to Seattle and on to Fairbanks with no problems.

Two days later our group arrived at Denali National Park. After a solid month of rain, the skies had cleared that morning, affording us a spectacular view of Mt. McKinley (now Mt. Denali) against a clear blue sky. The guide told us only a small percentage of visitors get to see the mountain at all, let alone with no clouds around it. The day we left, clouds once again moved in, shrouding the mountain from view. The highest peak in North America had truly burst forth before me.

As I shared the scripture with some of my travel companions, we rejoiced over the part about the mountains but assumed the part about the trees of the field was just a figure of speech. Then that afternoon on a covered wagon ride, our driver stopped the horses to let us listen to the wind blowing through the aspen trees. The rustling of their leaves sounded like an audience clapping their hands. God had just fulfilled that entire verse for me.

I realized that verse wasn't just a figure of speech, pretty words on a page, a poetic device. It was the almighty Creator of the universe using a physical sign in the natural world to confirm His written Word, assuring me of His involvement in my situation. I was excited and comforted at the same time by this precious reminder of His presence.

Before I ever left home, God knew what I was going to experience. *Now I declare new things; before they spring forth I proclaim them to you.* (Isaiah 43:19 NASB). Yes, He certainly did!

God Uses People

God's voice frequently comes to us through other people. He may use teachings, sermons, or the words of a friend or family member. Once we ask God for direction in a situation or need a specific question answered, we should listen. Frequently when a major issue or decision is involved, the message will be confirmed by coming through more than one source. *By the mouth of two or three witnesses every word shall be established* (2 Corinthians 13:1).

God also reveals truths we haven't specifically asked about. Something we read or hear may catch our attention; then it will seem we keep hearing the same thing over and over again, letting us know God is telling us something. Or the words of a song may seem to grab us. God's voice sometimes comes in unexpected ways – through a grocery store clerk, the person sitting behind us on the train, or a TV commercial. Once in the Old Testament, He even spoke through a donkey (Numbers 22:28-30). Sometimes no words will be involved at all. God simply draws our attention to a situation or person, such as the man who showed me how to work my windshield washer. When I saw him get out of a car just like mine and walk toward me, I didn't need a booming voice out of heaven saying, "Thou shalt ask that man!"

The Still, Small Voice

Most difficult to explain or describe in words is the *still, small voice* that comes to us on the inside. It may be very quiet and gentle, or the message can be so clear and plain it will almost sound like an audible voice in our head. The closest I ever came to hearing what seemed like God's audible voice was in 2004. Fifteen years earlier, after twenty-eight years of renting and never quite being able to afford to buy a home, Alan and I finally bought an old house for a very low price with a low interest rate for first-time homebuyers. It needed a lot of work. We spent eleven years there restoring the house to its original historic beauty. God blessed what we set our hands to (Deuteronomy 28:8), enabling us to sell it for almost four times what we had paid.

We used that money to buy a home closer to my work. The house was in a very expensive area, and when we bought it, we were financially stretched. Four years later I retired. Now, living on our pensions, we found ourselves having to take a little money out of savings each month to make ends meet. As you may have guessed, financial planning was not one of our stronger suits. As we prayed about our situation, we felt God was leading us to sell the house. With the improvements we had made on the home, we thought it should be worth more than we had paid, but we weren't sure how much more. We employed a realtor to appraise it and were delighted at the asking price she recommended. We told her we'd like to try selling it by owner for a couple weeks before listing it with her.

On the day we planned to put out the "For Sale" sign, Alan and I went out for our morning walk. As I was walking and praying quietly in the Spirit, I suddenly heard, very clearly and distinctly, "Don't set your sights too low."

"Lord?" I asked silently. The sentence was repeated.

"Alan, I think I just got a word from God."

"Really? What did He say?"

"He said not to set our sights too low."

"OK, then," Alan declared. "We won't."

This word from God encouraged us to ask more for the house than the realtor had recommended, reasoning that we could always come down if nothing happened. She had based her appraisal on what a regular homebuyer would likely be willing to pay. But God didn't send us a regular buyer; He sent a contractor. To him the zoning of the property made it worth every penny we were asking. Within two days we sold the house with no realtor and no yard sign. Even more amazing, the contractor turned right around at closing and sold the house to a group of real estate developers for $100,000 more than he had paid us!

Walking with God would certainly be easy if we always heard a clear, almost audible voice telling us what to do, but God wants us to be more sensitive and attentive than that. Usually, His voice will be stiller, smaller, and more subtle. He is calling us to a close, moment-by-moment relationship where we learn to know Him so well that we can hear His voice in the depth of our heart. This can only come with spending time in

His presence and seeking intimacy with Him. We can be sure God is always speaking to us, but listening is our responsibility. Think of a radio station that is broadcasting twenty-four hours a day. Radio waves are all around us, but only when we turn on the radio and tune in will we hear the program. We need to do the same with our spiritual receivers.

Developing attentiveness to God's voice involves both putting in and taking out. We amplify our spiritual hearing every time we put His truth into our heart by reading and speaking His Word, listening to teachings, singing scriptural songs, and using the power of our tongue to speak life. As we put truths into our heart, there is also a "taking out" process. We are surrounded by voices and thoughts that cause us to focus on sin, sickness, and all sorts of negative topics. These words and thoughts are speaking death. It is important to guard what we listen to, read, watch, and especially what we say. As we increase the input of life and truth into our hearts and decrease the input of death and lies, our spiritual ears will be quicker to perk up when God speaks.

Is It Really God?

When we hear a voice, how can we be sure it is our Shepherd's voice and not that of a stranger? Spending time with God and in His Word sharpens our ability to distinguish His voice from others. The better we know God's Word, the easier it becomes to identify thoughts or messages from other people – or our own mind – that do not line up with what He says. The closer our relationship becomes with God Himself and the more we experience His love, the better we come to know His character. Anything He tells us will speak of His mercy, grace, and love, and it will be consistent with His character.

Any word or thought that brings fear, condemnation, or doubt will not be from God. Any thought that makes us feel we need to do more to earn God's approval will not be from God. My plan for getting my life more organized was not from Him. I had listened to the voice of a stranger, probably my own flesh, saying, "I need to do more, I need to do better." Though the plan itself was not intrinsically bad and only consisted of doing good things, it was ungodly – and ineffective – because it was based on my works, not on faith in God's grace.

On my second morning in the Family House, I told God, "I'm Your sheep. Your Word says I know Your voice. I will not follow another." I expected to hear from Him. I didn't hear something every day; but having set my expectation to hear and recognize His voice, when I did hear it, I followed what He told me. Gradually this interaction became part of who I was. By the time Alan died, I had become one with God in a new way. This closeness with Him sustained me through some very difficult circumstances and helped me along the road as I moved into the next phase in my life.

I would like to encourage you, if you haven't yet begun to seek an intimate relationship with God, to consider getting started now. You don't have to wait till you are in a crisis situation to seek God with your whole heart. In fact, a close walk with God will strengthen you before a crisis hits. In many cases, if you are very attentive to His voice, He may lead you in ways that will avert a crisis altogether. God was undoubtedly trying to tell us Alan was in trouble long before we sought medical help, but we were not listening attentively. We ignored the still, small voice. Remember, part of listening involves acting on what we hear.

In order to enjoy this kind of intimacy with God, where we are able to hear and recognize His voice, we must first have a relationship with Him through Jesus Christ. If you have never taken this important first step, or you are not absolutely sure you have, you will find more information in the back of this book on the page titled "The First Step." If you have taken this step, then you can be assured that you *are* His sheep and you *can* hear His voice.

By listening to and following His voice, I was able to adjust to the responsibilities of running a household while also facing the challenge of finding a new home. With His help, I embarked on the next leg of my journey. Because of the close relationship I enjoyed with God, I was not afraid. I knew He held my future. I was eager to go where He wanted me to go and do what He called me to do. We are His sheep. We do hear his voice. We should expect to hear His voice. Whether through His Word, directly through other people, or deep within our heart through a still, small voice, we can be sure God is speaking to us. It brings Him great joy when we listen and respond.

5

Pause in the Action

Be still, and know that I am God. Psalm 46:10

My journey seemed to have screeched to a halt. After fifty-one years of traveling through life as Alan's wife, part of a unit joined together by God, suddenly I was just Judy. I didn't realize the extent to which this change of identity would impact every aspect of my life, but I did know I would need to make some major adjustments, and I knew I wasn't ready to move forward yet. Before I could proceed on my path as a "singled-out" woman, I needed to reassess, regroup, and pack a bag for the road ahead.

In the moments after Alan died, I was tired, numb, and barely functional. The whole experience simply didn't seem real. Julie and I mechanically stuffed Alan's clothing and my accumulation of paraphernalia into shopping bags and lugged them to the car. After the hospital staff removed the tubes, wires, and machines, we returned to the room and looked briefly at Alan's body. Then we looked at each other and said, "That isn't him."

For ten weeks the hospital had been my world, each day filled with concern over what was happening with Alan. Relationships with other families in the unit had been very important to me; we shared each other's triumphs and trials like family members. Just the day before I had been part of the cheering crowd when one family's daughter got up and walked down the hall for the first time after many long weeks of recovery. I had also felt strongly connected to certain staff members. Now, making the rounds to say my goodbyes, I felt like an alien there. Suddenly those people and events had no further connection with my life.

My daughter and I thanked the staff, grabbed the last few bags, and walked out of the hospital for the last time. Exhausted and too disoriented to attempt the long drive to my house, we headed for the Family House and wearily trudged up the stairs to my room. After sending a brief group e-mail telling our friends and family that Alan had gone home to be with the Lord, we went to bed. The Family House had been a place of refuge where I escaped each night and met with God each morning, but now it no longer felt like a haven. I needed to go home. The next morning Julie and I packed up our cars and headed there.

Home Again

During Alan's hospitalization, whenever I needed to return home without him, the house felt like an empty box. There was no comfort there for me. I would do what I needed to do and hurry back to be with him. Now, though, being at home felt good. Although Alan was not there with me, neither was he forty-five miles away, waiting for me to return to him. Now, seeing his chair, his clothes, and his belongings reassured me I was where I belonged.

Julie would be able to stay with me only one day. Neither of us was sure one day would be enough, but we had no choice.

The next day she and her family were flying to Florida for a spring break trip they had planned months before, and Doug and his family were leaving for Arizona. Not wanting either family to lose the money spent for deposits and airfare, I had encouraged them to proceed with their plans, postponing the date of the funeral to the following week. Julie and I used that day as productively as we could. Between visits and phone calls from neighbors, friends, and family, we restocked groceries, put away belongings from the hospital, and organized my life in general for the coming week.

When Julie left early Saturday morning, I didn't feel as if I was alone. I sensed God's presence. For several weeks He had been gently preparing me for this time; it didn't take Him by surprise. During our times together in the Family House, I had come to know Him better. Every day he had shown His loving care in the hospital by meeting my needs. Secure in His love, I had completely surrendered my future to Him just a few nights before; now that future was upon me. I had declared that I wouldn't be afraid, and I wasn't. Unsure of what to do next? Yes. But I wasn't unsure of my relationship with God. I could feel His presence in my heart and home.

I started the day just as I had done every morning at the Family House. I designated a chair for my "God time" and sat quietly, enjoying His company. After weeks of living on a bench in a hospital room and then in a room that offered peace and privacy but still wasn't my own, it was good to be home. After months of stress and concern over Alan's health, the long ordeal of ups and downs was over. Alan was gone, and that had been a shock; but knowing he was safe in heaven gave me comfort. Some have suggested I was in a state of denial, but I wasn't. I understood the reality of the circumstances, but I was also aware of a higher spiritual reality that trumped the circumstances.

That morning God enveloped me in unexplainable love and

peace. The apostle Paul called it *the peace that passes all under-standing* and *the love that surpasses knowledge* (Philippians 4:7; Ephesians 3:19). I'm so thankful I was able to develop a close walk with God *before* experiencing the loss of my husband. In the past, much lesser problems paralyzed me with fear, making me unable to function. Now, something truly terrible had happened, yet with a secure trust in God's goodness instead of being an emotional wreck, I was at peace – and functional.

After enjoying extra quiet time with God, I turned on my favorite worship music – loud! No longer having to worry about disturbing people around me, I sang along. I didn't know what lay ahead, but I was confident that whatever it was, God would handle it. I meant every word when I sang about His faithfulness. I felt God's peace as I sang songs about His presence dwelling in me. I rejoiced in the God who lifts me up on wings like eagles and strengthens me. Every song spoke truth to me about God and His goodness. I knew times of sadness would come, but this wasn't going to be one of them. I was spending quality time with the One who had promised He would never leave me or forsake me.

A Friend in Need

Next I made a quick assessment of the house, contemplating which job to tackle first. After my ten-week absence almost every room bore signs of the topsy-turvy lifestyle we led during Alan's illness, and there was dust on every horizontal surface. I had to put things back in order, but where to start? I was just pondering that when I received a phone call from our friend Mark in Colorado, whom we had met five years earlier through his job as partner representative for a ministry we supported. In those five years he had become a good friend. He had been a pillar of support throughout the time of Alan's illness, even coming to visit him once in the hospital.

Mark told me he had made reservations to come to the funeral, which I certainly had not expected. However, since that was going to be a really busy week for him, he wondered if he could come and visit this coming week instead. But, he said, he didn't want to infringe on our family time. "Well," I replied, "there isn't going to be any family time. They're all gone on their spring break vacations."

"What? You mean you're there alone?" he asked, incredulously.

"Sure, but I'll be fine. I have plenty to do, and I'm going to church tomorrow."

"By yourself?" Mark asked, surprised again.

"Yes, but I know a lot of people there. I'll find someone to sit with." I didn't really know a lot of people, but I didn't want Mark to worry about me.

"Well, I don't think you should be alone. Praise God, I'm coming today!"

Mark called later that morning to report that he had airline and hotel reservations and would be there to pick me up for church on Sunday morning. I don't know how my first day at home alone would have gone otherwise. The tasks facing me could have been overwhelming, and I might have given up before I even started. But needing to get ready for Mark's visit propelled me into action. No time to sit around and mope! I cranked up some Dixieland praise music and got to work, attacking dust and clutter until the downstairs began to look like its old self. Besides getting me moving, Mark's anticipated visit was a blessing to Doug and Julie. Concerned that I might not be quite ready to "fly solo" that first weekend, but unable to be there with me, they were relieved and delighted to know supportive companionship was on the way.

Sunday morning Mark arrived. After sharing a long hug and shedding a few tears, we headed for church. As we got out of the car, Mark said, "Okay, let's go in there and worship

Jesus!" I was ready! After ten weeks of hospital life, just being in church surrounded by God's people was wonderfully refreshing. When the music started, I began singing to the Lord with all my heart. Thankful for His goodness and love, I lifted my hands, heart, and voice to Him, and as I did, something truly amazing happened. Immersed in praise and worship, I felt a great, powerful surge of joy flooding into my heart. Despite the loss I had just experienced, despite all the uncertainty about the future, I encountered supernatural joy beyond anything I had ever experienced, flowing from somewhere deep inside of me.

In Your presence is fullness of joy; at Your right hand are pleasures forevermore (Psalm 16:11). I know this sounds strange. It may seem as if I've no clue what grief is all about. But the fullness of joy we find in God's presence makes no sense to human comprehension. It is not based on our circumstances. Like the peace that passes understanding, it is a gift, and God gave it to me that day. Instead of despair I was overcome with joy. He turned my mourning into dancing (Psalm 30:11). My soul was experiencing something much deeper and more substantial than mere happiness. Later, through all the trials and transitions I encountered in the process of becoming "just Judy," this genuine Holy Spirit joy remained within me, lifting me over many of the inevitable bumps in the road.

After church Mark invited Pastor Paul and his wife out to lunch, where we all reminisced about Alan and talked about the goodness of God. Then Mark and I spent the afternoon visiting my stepmother in the nursing home and running errands. I needed to make that visit and take care of those tasks anyway, but what a blessing not having to do them alone. We ended the afternoon with a light supper in a nearby restaurant and a trip to Walmart to pick up a few items my stepmother had asked for. God is awesome, and in His presence we're never alone; but that day I really appreciated the added presence of a caring human being. The next morning Mark came back and took me to breakfast before heading out of town. By then I was ready to face the coming week.

Mark's visit was a golden thread in a beautiful tapestry depicting God's love and tender care for me from the moment I made that 9-1-1 call. Throughout the weeks in the hospital, my children provided continual support. My sister called every day and twice came from California to stay with me. Friends, neighbors, and church people offered to help and came to visit. God also used people I hardly knew and even total strangers to meet needs, such as the man who helped with the windshield washer and the lady in the room next door who comforted me when Alan had his first septic episode. God usually put the help in place before I was even aware there would be a need.

Evidences of God's perfect timing were woven into that tapestry as well, such as Pastor Paul's arrival right before my meeting with the doctor. Right-place, right-time occurrences took place every day at the hospital. Now that I was home, it was clear God would continue to meet my needs, even going so far as sending Mark all the way from Colorado to Illinois to ease my transition. That was certainly *exceedingly abundantly above* all I could ask or think (Ephesians 3:20). I will never know the logistics involved in that plan; I just know Mark listened to God, and God used him to provide support when I needed it.

Regrouping

After Mark left, I resumed the process of organizing myself for the days ahead. Reading journal entries from that week, I'm amazed at all the activity: planning the funeral service and related events, getting the house back in order, gathering tax documents, and attending to financial concerns. I spent quality time with my stepmother, met with the pastors, the banker, and the lawyer, and took care of mail and phone calls.

It wasn't all business though. Friends took me out to lunch; I went to church on two evenings, and neighbors invited me to their house for dinner another night.

It was hard to get used to the fact that Alan was gone. For several weeks I would wake up each morning and glance over at his side of the bed to see if he was awake yet. The first few times it was a shock when I remembered why he wasn't there. On one of my first evenings at home, I was watching a TV show we had enjoyed together. The main character was in a tough spot, and the bad guy was sneaking up behind him. "Oh my gosh!" I exclaimed. "He doesn't see …" Then I glanced over toward Alan's chair and suddenly realized I was watching alone. Another time I missed what a character had said and asked Alan about it before remembering he wasn't there.

Staying by myself in the Family House eased the transition somewhat by giving me a taste of going to bed and getting up alone, but I was stunned by the abruptness of the change. I was Alan's wife one day and a single woman the next. My first days at home called for major adjustments in my thinking and activities. Suddenly I was head of the household. I moved into the new role with little fanfare. I didn't get to decide whether I wanted the job; I came home, and there it was. Each day brought challenges with decisions about things I never had to think about before, such as household maintenance and yard care. More than once I had to ask a neighbor to open a jar for me.

Overnight I became accountable for keeping track of the money. Thank goodness I knew how to use the computer to execute transactions, but it was Alan who had faithfully gone online every day and monitored the accounts. If some strange purchase showed up on our credit card account, he was right on top of it. Now I would be in charge of all that. Just as he had always put gas in the car, Alan had always told me when it was time to pay a bill or transfer funds. It was very embarrassing when I had a check returned for insufficient funds because I simply forgot to transfer money from savings to the checking account before writing a big check. Fortunately, that didn't happen during the first week!

Though some of the tasks and decisions were daunting, God helped me through each one. Sometimes He spoke directly to my heart, showing me what to do or whom to call. Other times He spoke through people: my sister, my children, friends, neighbors, even grocery clerks. He always provided the answers. I was able to face all that lay before me because of the relationship I had developed with Him. I knew I could place complete trust in Him and declare with assurance, "I will not be afraid" – He had removed all fear from my heart. Had it not been for that, I would have been a mess. The house and its strange noises would have been scary. Decisions would have overwhelmed me. I can't imagine how the old me could have taken on this new role.

The abrupt change in pace from the almost-frantic hospital scene to the quiet surroundings of my home could have been a recipe for depression and self-pity. The letdown reminded me of the way Alan and I always felt whenever the grandkids left after a long visit. Recognizing the feeling and not wanting to let it overpower me, I endeavored to keep myself occupied while also allowing time to rest and recover. I had been through a long, physically and emotionally draining struggle. But any time I found my mind wandering toward "would-a, could-a, should-a" thinking or drifting into the "what-ifs," I would turn on familiar praise and worship music and sing along. Praise and thanksgiving are powerful antidotes to all kinds of negative thoughts.

Living in the Bubble

My journal from that first week notes a few times when I was tired or feeling down, which is understandable, but my awareness of God's presence kept those moments from completely overpowering me. I now refer to those first few weeks as my time in the bubble. I moved through the days in a bubble of peace and love, where I seemed to be immune to many things that might ordinarily bother me. I felt like I was wrapped in a warm, soft blanket of well-being that cushioned me from fear, worry, and distress. Like a caterpillar in a cocoon, I was enclosed and protected from everyday cares while I gained inner strength. In the comfort of that bubble, I basked in the presence of God.

I think it is important to clarify one thing at this point. In looking at what happened to me during the time of Alan's hospitalization, a person might get the impression that I'm describing a ten-week crash course in getting to know God. It is true that the Judy who came out of that experience was certainly different from the one who called 9-1-1 ten weeks before. But the revelations I received from God during that time of growth were based on truths from His Word that I had been planting in my heart throughout the previous forty years. The Holy Spirit was teaching me by bringing to my remembrance those things I had read and heard over the years. He couldn't remind me of things I didn't already know.

God had been working in my life and answering my prayers for many years. I didn't go from total stranger to intimate relationship in a few weeks. Rather, by setting aside time every day to just be with Him and experience His presence, the truths I had been learning all those years were finally able to penetrate into a new place in my heart. I had opened myself to Him in a different way, allowing Him to bring our relationship to a deeper level of intimacy. In turn, He revealed those truths to me in a new and different way, applying them to my current situation.

Eventually the bubble feeling began to fade, but by that time my close bond with God was well established, and I was able to trust Him without being thrown off course by every little problem that arose. In speaking with other widows, I've learned that my experience was not terribly unusual. The bubble seems to be a special gift God often provides to cushion the blow of a spouse's death, and it was a wonderful blessing to me, especially that first week.

Despite the bubble, there were a few tough moments, such as my trip to the mall to buy a new dress for the funeral. I would have been happy to wear the dress I had always relied upon for special occasions, but it no longer fit, forcing me to buy a new one. Having a general idea of what I needed, I blithely jumped in the car and drove to the mall. Finding something that seemed suitable, I took it to the fitting room. Usually when purchasing an important piece of clothing, I took Alan along for feedback, but of course now I couldn't do that. So I switched to Option B, walking out onto the sales floor to consult a clerk or another customer.

But how could I ask a complete stranger, "Excuse me, do you think this dress would be appropriate for my husband's funeral?" A stab of heaviness squeezed my chest and left me almost breathless. I finally asked someone if they thought the dress fit properly but didn't mention the word *funeral*, not wanting to open up that conversation with someone I didn't know. Feeling burdened as if I had a terrible secret I didn't feel comfortable sharing and nearly immobilized by the crushing sense of utter aloneness, I returned to the fitting room, changed back into my clothes, and bought the dress. No friendly chatting with sales clerks that day.

By the time I returned home, I had recovered. But I was annoyed with myself not to have realized this shopping trip might be loaded with emotional dynamite. I could easily have asked someone to go with me – someone who would know what the dress was for and could help me with the selection.

After that experience, I tried to anticipate and avoid situations that might bring on feelings of grief and loss. They were bound to come often enough without my sending them an engraved invitation. Though I couldn't foresee every emotional trigger, I learned to minimize them by being on alert.

Having more than a week to prepare myself for the funeral undoubtedly helped me stay calm and composed. During this time I was able to move beyond the initial shock of the loss before facing a room full of people. In those first few days, God gave me peace that passes understanding, unspeakable joy, and the comfort of His presence. He used the people around me to meet my needs. He demonstrated that He could be trusted.

I wasn't afraid to face the road ahead, but it wasn't yet time to embark on the next phase of my journey. I was still catching my breath. I had grown in my understanding of who I was and what I had in Christ, but before proceeding I also had to figure out who I was and what I had in practical terms. During this brief sojourn, as I gathered my spiritual and material resources for the next leg of the trip, God held me up, held me close, and held me together. I rested in that bubble of comfort and closeness and kept my mind stayed on Him. All the work He had been doing in my heart those last few weeks was bearing the fruit of love, joy, and peace that would sustain me when it was time to venture forth on the new adventures He was weaving into the tapestry of my life.

6

A New Road Ahead

*Trust in the LORD with all your heart, and lean
not on your own understanding; in all your ways
acknowledge Him, and He shall direct your paths.*
Proverbs 3:5-6

At home, free from the distractions of hospital life, I was
able to spend more quality time alone with God. Naturally,
I wondered what life might have in store for me in this new
phase. I was not afraid. All traces of fear left the night I made
the commitment to trust God no matter what, but I did wonder. There was no hurry to make changes; I had plenty to do
preparing for the funeral and trying to make sense of all the
loose ends in my life. In Jeremiah 29:11 God says He has a plan
for us, and it is good. I believed when the time was right, He
would reveal His thoughts and plans. I was very surprised,
however, at how quickly He began the process.

In the middle of my very first week alone, even before the
funeral had taken place, God spoke to me through a passage
in the book of Isaiah. A melody had been going through my

mind that morning. Knowing it was the tune to Isaiah 43:1-3, I decided to skip my plan and read that instead. But before I got there, another passage caught my eye. As I read it, I was riveted. *I am the Lord, I have called You in righteousness, I will also hold Your hand and watch over You* (Isaiah 42:6 NASB). That was exactly what I needed to hear. Wow! I was truly alone for the first time in my life, yet God was assuring me that I would not be alone. He would continue to hold my hand and watch over me. He had my attention.

Then in the following verses, He revealed His purpose for the next phase of my life: *I will appoint You as a covenant to the people, as a light to the nations, to open blind eyes, to bring out prisoners from the dungeon and those who dwell in darkness from the prison. I am the Lord, that is My name; I will not give My glory to another, nor My praise to graven images. Behold, the former things have come to pass, now I declare new things; before they spring forth I proclaim them to You* (Isaiah 42:6-9 NASB).

Reading that passage, I felt joyful anticipation welling up in my heart. Although I realized this was a prophetic Scripture in which God was talking about Jesus, I felt He was also speaking directly to me, because the final words about leaving the past and moving into new things for the future related so specifically to my immediate circumstances. The passage also gave me a hint about my future. Eventually, I would have a role in His kingdom that would somehow involve opening blind eyes and freeing prisoners. He was promising that before new things happened, He would let me know what was coming. Naturally, I didn't expect Him to spell out day-by-day and week-by-week plans for me, but how reassuring it was to know He would keep me posted along the way. Several times that day and the next, I picked up the Bible and read the passage again, thanking Him for speaking to me.

Two days later, another passage jumped out at me bearing

a similar message: *Do not call to mind the former things, or ponder things of the past. Behold, I will do something new, now it will spring forth; will you not be aware of it? I will even make a roadway in the wilderness, rivers in the desert* (Isaiah 43:18-19 NASB). The similarity between God's instructions and promises in these two passages reinforced my belief that this was what God wanted me to do: forget the former things of my old life and get ready for the new things He had prepared for me.

My first question was – how do I obey the instruction to not call to mind the former things or ponder the past? The former things were still very fresh in my mind. My husband had just died. Did God want me to forget him and disregard our fifty-one years of life together? I didn't think so. In fact, that previous summer with our family, Alan and I had celebrated our fiftieth anniversary with a big party. My sister and her whole family had come from California and Arizona, and many other family members attended, as well as former high school classmates and people we had worked with over the years. In preparation for that God had put a strong desire in my heart to make a scrapbook depicting our first fifty years.

I had pulled out all my boxes of photos and documented our entire life together, beginning with our first date. The monumental project took more than three months of day-in, day-out work and ended up being much larger than I had anticipated – five hefty volumes. As I completed each one, Alan would sit and read the whole thing, sometimes chuckling, sometimes shedding a tear. We read those books and looked at those pictures many times before and after the party, and they brought us comfort and encouragement right up until the night we found ourselves in the hospital.

Now, as I contemplated the two scriptures telling me not to ponder the former things, I thought of those scrapbooks and the photos from our anniversary party. Why would God put a desire in my heart to record all those memories if I was supposed to just forget about everything that had gone before? No, that was not what He meant. Remembering the past can be a valuable activity. Happy memories warm the heart and remind us of God's love and care for us. Even thinking of less happy times can be helpful if we remember the lessons we learned through them. And remembering things God has done for us in the past helps build our faith in our current situation.

On the other hand, there is danger in spending too much time thinking about things of the past, which is why God tells us not to ponder them. According to the *Merriam-Webster Dictionary, ponder* means "to weigh in the mind; deliberate over." Many thoughts came to my mind, especially in the early days, which could have dragged me down had I entertained them for any length of time. Thoughts such as *maybe we should have done this differently,* or *maybe we shouldn't have done that. What if we had tried this treatment, or gone to a different doctor, or gone sooner? If only ...* Pondering such thoughts can be very destructive. Some of those times in the hospital were just plain awful. There was nothing to be gained by reliving them. As God says, the former things have come to pass. They are finished. Getting bogged down in trying to figure them out after the fact serves no useful purpose and can lead to condemnation and discouragement.

Letting Go of Former Things

Near the end of the week, I sent a group e-mail update to friends and family, including this loving tribute to Alan:

> *Of course I miss Alan terribly, and I think about him all the time. It's quite an adjustment. We always did everything together, so even a trip to Walmart feels a little funny by myself. But I'm not*

worried about Alan. I know for certain where he is, and Who he's with. Although I don't know exactly what he's doing, I know that he is enjoying it. He is no longer sick, tired, or worried.

He was a godly man who believed strongly in God's Word and tried to live according to it. He was a wonderful husband, father, grandfather, friend, and neighbor. I am just beginning to discover what an influence he had on many people's lives. He had a close relationship with God, and he wanted to share that with everyone. He also wanted to share with other believers the things he was learning in the Word that he thought would help them. When someone wasn't able to understand or receive what he was trying to share, he would become very frustrated, and sometimes the way he handled that frustration made it hard for the person to realize that he was motivated by love, but he was.

When he took on a task, whether it was caring for the yard, redecorating or remodeling a room, or organizing the garage, he was diligent and persistent. Realizing now that for much of that time he really didn't feel well (but of course never told anyone), it is even more amazing to look back on all that he accomplished. He really got a kick out of leaving things better than the way he had found them. He took pride in his work, but was always quick to add that it was God who had shown him how to do things and who had blessed him with houses to work on and the talent to see how something was really supposed to look, and then get it to look that way.

*He loved to sit on the front porch or in the fam-
ily room, looking out the window, or on the couch,
watching all the family and house photos on the
screen saver. He called this "counting my blessings."
He marveled at how awesomely God had blessed us.
I marvel at it, too.*

Although at the time I didn't recognize it as such, writing that
tribute was an important step in letting go of the past and moving forward. Making that statement released me emotionally
to shift my focus toward the future.

More Closure

The funeral is always an important part of the closure process.
By having this service, we are not saying goodbye so we can walk
away and forget the loved one. The grieving process doesn't end
when we drive away from the gravesite. My memories of Alan
will always be with me, and I will think about him for the rest
of my life; he is a permanent part of who I am and who I will
become. But we do need to reach a place where our heart is at
peace with the past and we are ready to move into the future.
I worked with the pastors to plan a funeral service that would
help all of us do that by celebrating Alan's life and his walk
with the Lord, while bringing glory to the goodness of God.

As I worked on the preparations, it was hard to get it through
my head that we really were saying goodbye. It was sad knowing Alan would not get to watch his grandchildren grow up.
He had told the heart surgeon he wanted to live long enough
to see, as he put it, what they turned out to be. But I didn't
want the service to focus on the sadness or the loss. I wanted
it to emphasize what Alan had accomplished and how he had
touched other people's lives.

In addition to planning details of the visitation, service,

and lunch, I had to prepare for the trip to the Chicago area where everything was to take place. Doug would pick me up on Monday morning, and I would stay at his house. In typical female fashion, I set about choosing, and changing my mind about, clothes and jewelry to bring. I had the dress for the funeral, of course, and had selected a pair of nice black dress pants and a sweater set for the visitation. Not sure what jewelry I should wear with the dress, I packed two sets, as well as clothes for the rest of my time there and all the other items one packs. After deciding and redeciding, arranging and rearranging, I was ready to roll when Doug arrived to pick me up.

On Tuesday, Doug and I spent the morning meeting with funeral home and cemetery representatives, followed by a leisurely lunch with his wife, Joanne, before returning to their house to get ready for the visitation. I showed Joanne my dress for the funeral and sought her advice on the jewelry. Then just on a whim, which I attribute to a nudge from God, I asked, "Would you like to see what I'm wearing for the visitation?" I pulled out the sweater set, and to my horror discovered that the pants were not there! I had left them hanging on the closet door at home. And the visitation would be starting in two hours.

I know people who have seen visions of angels or even of Jesus. I never have. But that day I did see a vision of me at the funeral parlor standing bare-legged while greeting a room full of people – and it wasn't pretty! Because God had tipped me off about my omission two hours before I needed the pants, we had time to go to the store and buy a new pair without rushing or getting into a panic. The first store we went to had exactly what I needed, further evidence that God was indeed holding me by the hand. His timing was perfect, and once again He had already provided for a need I didn't even know I had.

The visitation went very smoothly. Fully clothed, I enjoyed seeing all the friends and family members who came. The service the next day was the celebration of Alan's life I had hoped for, a wonderful tribute to his many good qualities and the impact he had on other people's lives. Although we were gathered for a sad occasion, it was not depressing because we all knew Alan had gone to be with Jesus, and we would be joining him again someday. Even so, it was hard to wrap my mind around the fact that he was really gone.

When I returned home the following day, Julie, Doug, and Joanne came along to help start the sorting out process. Alan and I had a two-story home with many years of accumulation. As I had promised him, I planned to move to the north suburbs of Chicago near my kids and grandkids as soon as possible and would not need or have room for most of our belongings. This was another part of letting go of former things. I was pretty sure I wouldn't need fourteen power drills or six vacuum cleaners. (Alan liked the idea of having a back-up in case something broke down!) Although it would take two big garage sales and many charitable donations to enable me to downsize, we made a good start in clearing out the garage and basement.

I Will Do Something New

Even as I worked on laying aside the former things, as God had promised, some new things began to emerge for the future. A couple days after the kids left, my sister called from California. She was planning to visit and help me get ready for my first garage sale and a memorial open house. We decided after all this we ought to do something together just for fun. I was contemplating a trip to Colorado Springs in July to attend a Bible conference, followed by driving to the Denver area for a cousin's wedding. We thought it would be fun for her to join me at the conference and then drive with me to the wedding. The trip would be a new experience for me. I hadn't been on an airplane since the 1990s.

In these early stages of being singled out, whenever I needed to make an important decision, I strongly considered what I thought Alan would say. Throughout my forty years of being a Christian, one of the ways I heard from God was by asking Him to speak through my husband. This worked very well when Alan was living, and after fifty-one years of marriage I had a pretty good idea what he was likely to say about most things, so I continued to consider his wisdom and opinions. I think this is an excellent policy for women who are newly singled out. I'm sure this approach kept me from doing bizarre, out-of-character things as I gradually transitioned to making my own decisions. Alan and I had wanted to attend that annual Bible conference for several years, so I was sure he would have approved of my travel plans.

As I began moving into the new things God had in store for me, I continued to include what Alan might have thought as part of my decision-making process, and I believe if he could look on my life even now, he would be very pleased with the decisions I've made. He would be just as surprised as I've been to see all the new things that would be springing forth for me on the new road ahead.

7

Opening Blind Eyes

Therefore, if anyone is in Christ, he is a new creation; old things have passed away; behold, all things have become new. 2 Corinthians 5:17

A s I went through the process of letting go of the past, I continued to meditate on the verses God had given me in Isaiah 42:7. His promise to hold me by the hand and watch over me brought great comfort, and I was thrilled that He had new things planned for me. But beyond these general assurances, He had given me a more specific word about His plan and purpose for the rest of my life. *And I will appoint you as a covenant to the people, as a light to the nations, to open blind eyes, to bring out prisoners from the dungeon, and those who dwell in darkness from the prison* (Isaiah 42:6-7 NASB).

"Lord," I asked, "I know there are many kinds of blindness, and they aren't all physical. Am I going to have a ministry of healing blind people, or does this mean something else? Also, what are the dungeons and prisons You're talking about?" I realized Isaiah was originally writing about Jesus, telling the

Jewish people that the new covenant was for the nations – all people, not just for the Jews. But God showed me how the passage also applied to me personally.

"My body," He said, "is full of precious people who are not able to receive all I have for them because they are blind to who they are in Me. They are imprisoned by their wrong thinking and kept in darkness by their misunderstanding of My Word. I want to use you to help them." How I would be doing this was not clear, but at the time it was enough to know the general direction of His plan.

I could certainly relate to spiritual blindness. For thirty years Alan and I stumbled in darkness, blind to who we were in Christ. We had been saved and baptized in the Holy Spirit in 1972 while living in Kansas City. Our marriage and our lives before that had not been good. We were both immature and self-centered, and neither of us had a clue what a husband or wife was supposed to act like. Soon after accepting Jesus, we saw our attitudes change and our marriage became better. Not perfect, but much better. Happy to know our sins had been forgiven, we enthusiastically attended church and a weekly share group where we prayed with others and grew together with them in our understanding of the Word.

The preaching we heard in those days came right out of the Bible. It was primarily focused on how to be better people, better mates, better parents, and better employees. Generally, the pastor would expound on a topic, honesty for example. He would share Scriptures about why honesty was important and the consequences of being dishonest. He would illustrate the topic using a character from the Bible or from personal experience. The sermon would typically end with a prayer that God would help all of us to be more honest. The pastor encouraged anyone who was really struggling with the problem to come up to the altar for prayer. We would leave church determined to make a greater effort.

We also heard many sermons on how to become better Christians: pray longer, read the Bible more, be sure to confess every sin to get it "under the blood," and, of course, serve faithfully in the church. We heard sermons on the need to die to ourselves – "More of Jesus, less of me" – and the importance of putting on our spiritual armor. There was no shortage of dos and don'ts. We really desired to live lives pleasing to God, but sometimes it was frustrating. It seemed as if no matter how we tried, we could never quite do enough.

In 1976, Alan was transferred to Chicago, and we moved to a North Shore suburb. We continued trying to do all the things good Christians are supposed to do: pray, read the Bible, go to church, tithe, confess, and serve. We read the Bible all the way through – both silently and aloud – many times, and the New Testament many more times. Somehow, though, our Christian walk felt like a long, uphill climb. As Paul describes in Romans 7:15-23, we knew the right things to do and wanted to do them but found ourselves doing the things we didn't want to do. We weren't stealing, committing adultery, or cheating on our taxes. We just weren't the people God wanted us to be.

So, what was wrong with us? The problem was that we didn't understand our identity in Christ. While the teaching we had been hearing came from the Bible, it had been incomplete. The emphasis had been on what *we* should do, not on the work the Holy Spirit could accomplish *in* us. The focus was on our performance rather than on what Jesus had done *for* us. We were blinded to several important spiritual truths, and this ignorance was crippling our Christian walk. Fortunately, in 2003, God opened our spiritual eyes, and our lives took a turn for the better.

Our Eyes Are Opened

When I retired from my career as a high school teacher, we decided to read something worthwhile every day in addition to the Bible. We enjoyed reading aloud to each other, alternating chapters. We started reading a book about Galatians our daughter had given us. We hadn't gone very far before Alan said, "If we're going to read *about* Galatians, maybe we should go back and read Galatians itself again, just to refresh our memory." So we did. Then we decided we would also read Ephesians since it is such an encouraging book. When we came to Ephesians 1:17-20, Alan said, "You know, this is a pretty good prayer. Maybe we should pray it for ourselves."

So we prayed what Paul wrote, asking God, the glorious Father of our Lord Jesus Christ, to give us spiritual wisdom and understanding, so that we might grow in our knowledge of Him. We prayed that our hearts would be flooded with light, so we could understand the wonderful future He has promised to those He called, that we would realize what a rich and glorious inheritance he has given to His people, and that we would begin to understand the incredible greatness of His power for us who believe Him. Every day we prayed that prayer, and I must say, it is a pretty good prayer, because within a few days God began to answer it.

First, we received a book from a cousin explaining the basic message of salvation more clearly than we had ever heard it. As we pondered the truths of the gospel outlined in that book, we also happened across a minister on TV who was teaching from Romans on "The Gospel, the Power of God." Since his teaching lined up with what we had been reading, it captured our interest, and that program became a part of our daily routine.

Our spiritual eyes were opened. Here was the missing link in our understanding of God. We saw we had been getting the whole thing backwards. All these years, we had been trying to do all the right things to earn God's approval, when in reality, as soon as we gave our lives to Christ in 1972, we *had* his approval. His love for us was not based on anything we had done or could do, but on the finished work of Jesus Christ on the cross. Understanding this truth made all the difference.

It's easy to see why many Christians don't understand God's love and grace. The entire world system is performance based. From the time we are small children, we learn that if you want to be rewarded you have to be good. When you're not so good, either you receive punishment or the reward is withheld. Our experiences with parents, teachers, and bosses reinforce this concept. Even in relationships, such as marriage or friendship, we need to comply with expectations in order to receive. So, no wonder then, when we come into the kingdom of God, unless someone has done a really good job of explaining grace to us, we interact with God assuming He operates the same way.

As we grew in our understanding of God's unconditional love and grace, we continued to do the same things as before. We still read our Bibles, but we enjoyed it more. Instead of viewing the Bible as a set of instructions on how to live, we saw it as a picture of God's love for us and a description of all the things we had in Him. We still prayed, but now instead of spending most of the time confessing our sins and asking for forgiveness, we thanked God that He has already forgiven us. Praying this way changed the focus away from ourselves and our sins to Jesus and what He has done for us. No longer trying to earn God's approval, we enjoyed life more. As Alan said, he no longer felt as if God was just waiting for a chance to drop a piano on his head if he got out of line – an exaggeration for sure, but it did illustrate the new freedom we felt.

A New Creation? Are You Kidding?

And speaking of exaggerations, look at this Bible verse: *Therefore, if anyone is in Christ, he is a new creation; old things have passed away; behold, all things have become new* (2 Corinthians 5:17). Is God kidding? That verse always puzzled me. Although I loved the idea of being new, I wasn't convinced I really was a new creation. Oh, through the years God had smoothed some rough edges and many of my attitudes had improved, but was I a *new* creation? How could that be? I still had many of my old habits. I still slipped easily into pity party mode when things didn't go my way. I had a long way to go in the process of becoming *conformed to the image of His Son* (Romans 8:29).

So, was God exaggerating when He said we were a new creation? This mystery was solved when once again God opened my spiritual eyes, and I began to understand the difference between the soul and the spirit. We are composed of three parts: spirit, soul, and body (1 Thessalonians 5:23). I knew that, but I didn't realize that when we are born again, only our spirit is changed. It is brand new and is perfect forever. In our spirit, we are exactly like Jesus. Our spirit never sins. But the other two parts? That's a different story.

Our body is obviously not a new creation. One look in the mirror tells us that. But what about the soul? I always assumed it was the soul that was saved, but that isn't accurate. I thought the terms *soul* and *spirit* were basically interchangeable, but in reality they are two distinctly different parts of us. The soul consists of our mind, will, and emotions – all of those non-physical parts that make us who we are. We could say the soul is actually another word for our personality. The moment we accepted Christ, our spirit was born again. We became a new creation, one with the Holy Spirit. Our soul, though, is not born again. It must be transformed through the renewing of our mind (Romans 12:2).

The renewing of our mind doesn't happen immediately or automatically. It is a process that can go fast or slow depending on choices we make. This is why Bible study is so important. The Word of God tells us who we are in Christ. And here is great news: This is how God sees us! He looks at our spirit, and He sees the righteousness of God (2 Corinthians 5:21). That's why He is able to love us unconditionally – because when He looks at us, He sees the righteousness of Jesus. Understanding the relationship between the spirit and the soul truly unlocked the Scriptures for me. Seen through the framework of a born-again spirit, perfect and complete, and a soul that is gradually being transformed by the renewing of the mind, the whole New Testament suddenly made sense.

What Does God Want from Us?

Being able to see that God's love for us didn't depend on our performance was wonderfully freeing. Understanding that we truly are a new creation, even though it may not be outwardly visible, made reading the Bible more like a treasure hunt than another lecture. But during my time in the Family House, my spiritual eyes were opened to an even more important truth: God's primary goal is not to improve us. Does that surprise you? For almost forty years I thought that was what the Christian walk was all about, letting God work on us, and in us, to make us more like Jesus.

But if God doesn't want to improve us, then what *does* He want? The answer to this question is the most beautiful truth in the entire Bible: God's deepest desire is to be in relationship with us. He started mankind's life on earth that way. Before they sinned, Adam and Eve had an intimate relationship with God. After the Fall, God immediately began putting the pieces in place for sending Jesus to redeem us. Sin had separated us from Him, and He wanted to bring us back into relationship. That relationship is so important to Him that He sent His precious Son to die on the cross, because that was the only way He could remove the barrier sin had placed between us.

We are all familiar with John 3:16: *For God so loved the world that He gave His only begotten Son, that whoever believes in Him should not perish but have everlasting life.* As a general rule, we translate it to say: God loved us so much that He sent Jesus to die for us so we won't perish or go to hell. Of course, it does say that, and that is awesome, but the really important part of the verse is the last four words: *but have everlasting life.* Most people view this as a continuation of the "should not perish" part: we won't go to hell when we die; we'll go to heaven.

Although this is true, it is only part of the truth. There is so much more. Everlasting life does not begin after we die; it begins the moment we're born again. In His prayer on the night before His crucifixion, Jesus defined it. *And this is eternal life, that they may know You, the only true God, and Jesus Christ whom You have sent* (John 17:3). The word *know* used here is the same word that was used in Genesis 4:1 where it says Adam knew his wife, Eve, and she conceived a child. You can't get more intimate than that! The purpose of Jesus' death on the cross was to remove the separation between God and man, so He could once again have a relationship with us. Now that Jesus has paid the price for our sin, by accepting His sacrifice we are free to enter into intimacy with God.

When we draw closer and closer to Him, an amazing thing happens: As with any other friend, when we hang out with God, we begin taking on His mannerisms and seeing things from His point of view. We really don't need to worry about improving ourselves because the Holy Spirit will gently lead, correct, and change us. We will find our desires changing so that things we used to do that weren't in our best interest will lose their appeal. We will find ourselves effortlessly becoming more like Jesus. *For God is working in you, giving you the desire to obey him and the power to do what pleases him* (Philippians 2:13 NLT).

What God really wants is simply to be with us. Understanding this frees us to go about our day without fear of falling short, missing the mark, or making Him mad. I love to start each day quietly waiting to hear from Him. Throughout the day I talk to Him and listen for His voice. Some days I am very aware of His presence. Other days I may not feel at all connected. But He has promised He will never leave or forsake us, so I know He's there (Hebrews 13:5). Imagine your conversation with Him at the end of a day spent in His presence: "Thank You, Lord, for all of the blessings You gave me today," you say.

And then you hear a quiet inner voice saying, "You really blessed Me today, too. I loved it when you were humming that song and thinking about Me. It was fun opening up that great parking space for you. And I so enjoyed being allowed to speak through you in that conversation with your friend."

Yes, He desires intimate relationship with us. He longs for it. I had a pretty clear understanding of grace versus works for at least ten years, and I could explain the relationship between our soul and spirit as well. But after all those years of skirting the edge of the path, I finally embarked on a deeper, closer walk with God. It was a lot like coming home from a long trip, sitting back, and putting my feet up, only it wasn't physical. In that deep, quiet place where my heart communed with God, I could sense a uniting of my soul and spirit. As the truths I already understood became clearer, I began to look and act more like who I am in the spirit. The renewing of my mind was beginning to bear fruit.

8

A Roadway in the Wilderness

You will show me the path of life; in Your presence is fullness of joy; at your right hand are pleasures forevermore. Psalm 16:11

As I spent time in God's presence, secure in the above Scripture promise, He began to reveal my path of life and I continued to walk in joy. I had taken steps to let go of the former things and was making every effort not to ponder the past. The two passages in Isaiah had encouraged me and strengthened my faith. *Now I declare new things; before they spring forth I proclaim them to you* (Isaiah 42:9 NASB). *Behold, I will do something new, now it will spring forth; will you not be aware of it? I will even make a roadway in the wilderness, rivers in the desert* (Isaiah 43:19 NASB). Both passages were full of promise for my future. I didn't know how or when these "new things" would come about, but it was clear that long before I knew this bend in the road was coming, God had been preparing me for the next steps of my journey. Now I was walking securely with God holding me by the hand, eager for whatever new things He wanted to do. I typed out both, including the part about the blind eyes and prisons, and attached them to my refrigerator door.

A week or so later, a high school classmate sent me a very encouraging condolence e-mail. Here is part of what she wrote: "Your life has taken a sharp turn as well as the lives of Doug and Julie and all their children. However, the One who walks with all of you knows your pain, and He holds you close to His heart. May all of you live with the sweet memories of your full life with Alan. The dark night of uncertainty is over, and you have indeed 'passed through the waters.' You are on the other side. Now, after a time the Lord says, *Behold, I will do a new thing, now it shall spring forth; shall you not know it? I will even make a road in the wilderness and rivers in the desert* (Isaiah 43:19)."

There was "my" passage again. I hadn't known this classmate very well and had no idea she was even reading my e-mails. She most certainly knew nothing about the scripture God had given me; I had not shared it with anyone yet. The following Wednesday evening before Bible study at church, I did share it with a friend, explaining how God had first drawn me to it and now confirmed it through this e-mail. Imagine how my heart jumped when, an hour later during our Bible study, the pastor's wife used that same verse in her lesson. She was not aware of what God had shown me. Now the promise had been confirmed twice! I was so thrilled about hearing from God so clearly that I had a hard time sitting still and being quiet through the rest of that Bible study.

Meanwhile, I continued seeking God at the beginning of each day, enjoying His presence and basking in His love. In almost no time He led the way to a new place to live. I got rid of things I couldn't use, packed up, and moved to the Chicago suburbs. It all happened so fast I didn't really have time to process what God was doing at the time. I just asked Him for wisdom each day, did what needed to be done, and kept moving forward. Now as I look back at how perfectly God put everything together, I can see the steps I followed. There is no magic formula for finding God's will, but He has set forth principles in His Word. If we follow them, we will end up where He wants us to be.

A Roadway in the Wilderness

The scriptures in Isaiah were on my refrigerator, on my mind, and frequently spoken with my mouth. What the pastor's wife had said about the passage really touched me. She had emphasized the part where God promised to make roadways in the wilderness and rivers of water in the desert. She drew a vivid word picture of water springing up in the middle of the desert. To me this meant He would lead me to my new home, and I believed the rivers referred to the living water of the Holy Spirit. With my new home would come a church or other group of believers where I would find spiritual refreshment. I went forth into that wilderness with great expectations.

The area where I was going was not a physical wilderness, but to me it might as well have been because I didn't know my way around there. Other than a general idea of living near my kids and renting at first rather than buying a home, I didn't know what would be best for me. I was like a stranger in a foreign land. I thanked God for His promise to make a roadway there for me and left the driving to Him. When all was said and done, less than three months after walking out of that hospital, I was moving into a condo near my family that was perfect for me, a place where new blessings would spring forth each day. Within a few more weeks I found spiritual refreshment as well.

Stepping into the Unknown

The steps I followed can be applied to almost any journey into unknown territory. Step number one is to know what God says about the situation. In my case, I focused on two scriptural facts. First, when Jesus went to be with the Father, He said He was going to prepare a place for us in heaven (John 14:3). Second, He instructed us to pray, *Your kingdom come. Your will be done, on earth as it is in heaven* (Matthew 6:10 NASB). By combining these two truths, I concluded that just as He has prepared a permanent place for me in heaven, He had also prepared a temporary place for me here on earth in the Chicago suburbs. I also had the promise in Isaiah that He would make a roadway in the wilderness.

Once we have God's Word on the subject, it's time to activate our faith. Faith is the connector that brings spiritual reality from God's Word into manifestation here on earth. We activate it with our words. Just as God created the whole natural world and everything in it by spoken words, we who are made in His image and likeness also bring things into being through our spoken words. We don't create new things, but as our words line up with the truth in God's Word, we release those spiritual truths into our lives.

I was careful to guard my tongue. I'll talk more about the importance of watching what we say later, but I mention it now because it is an important step in this process. I kept thanking God for His promises. When discouraging or scary thoughts would come, I didn't empower those thoughts by giving them voice. I only spoke what God's Word said: God has a place for me; He is my provider; He has made a roadway for me in the wilderness.

Words activate our faith, but the Bible also tells us that faith without works is dead (James 2:17). We must back up our words with actions. I didn't sit around thinking nice thoughts, saying faith-filled words, idly waiting for God to drop an address into my head out of the blue. After checking out housing possibilities online, I contacted a realtor and explained my needs. I told her I would be coming up there the following weekend to see my grandson in a play and would like to look at several places while I was in the area to get the lay of the land and to help her get a sense of my likes and dislikes.

Actions show that we believe what we're saying. In addition to making arrangements for looking at possible new homes, I began making a diligent effort to get rid of things I wouldn't need in this new phase of my life. "I'm going to be moving soon," I told people, "so I need to get rid of all this stuff." Paring down from a very full four-bedroom house to a two-bedroom condo was a challenge, but it was a great opportunity to bless others – giving things away or selling them at bargain prices. Lots of men in our community went away from the garage sales happily laden with power tools, yard equipment, and every kind of gadget imaginable.

Soon I ventured forth on my weekend in the suburbs near my kids' homes. As I looked at various townhomes, every place that seemed it might work was rented to someone else before I could give it serious thought. Several places came on the market, only to be rented before I even had a chance to see them. The realtor said, "The rental market up here is hot right now." We looked all weekend to no avail. The weekend was a success in that I had a great time with the grandchildren, but the rental market turned out to be more of a wilderness than I had expected. Because properties were going so quickly, it seemed I would need to move fast if something I liked did become available. A sense of urgency came over me that I didn't have when I left home, and I didn't see how I could get the job done from two hundred miles away.

A Place Prepared for Me

By Sunday afternoon, just when it seemed we were back to square one, my daughter thought of another nearby suburb where we hadn't looked. She also suggested I consider an apartment in a condo building instead of a townhouse. I was hesitant at first but decided I could at least take a look at a few. Monday morning the realtor showed us three. Each had some major drawback. The third place was in a nice building, but I didn't care for the unit itself.

As we walked back into the hallway, the realtor said, "There is another unit for rent in this building, but I haven't been able to get ahold of the listing agent. Shall I try calling once more?" We didn't have much time; I had a train to catch. But we were already there, so I said yes. Voila! The minute I entered that apartment it felt like me, exceeding my every hope and expectation. It had many features I had resigned myself to giving up when I downsized, and the floor plan was configured perfectly to accommodate my needs. I could picture my furniture there. This was amazing, miraculous!

So, of course I said, "I'll take it!" right? Well, although I'm embarrassed to admit it, the great faith I had been continually and confidently declaring suddenly seemed to evaporate. As the enormity of the decision hit me, thoughts came bouncing into my mind. *What if I make a mistake? I don't want to be stuck in a place that isn't where God wants me.* Everything looked good on the surface, but maybe there were factors I didn't know about that could cause problems later. It's said that when something seems too good to be true it usually is. I was determined that I would be led by the peace of God (Colossians 3:15). At that moment I didn't feel peace; I felt panicky.

"So?" asked the realtor. I shrugged my shoulders. She and my daughter looked at me as if to say, "Are you crazy?"

"I'm sorry," I told them. "I just can't do it." I couldn't make a decision on the spot. I knew how quickly rental units were being snatched up, but with this uneasy feeling, I was afraid to commit. I had completed a rental application just in case I found something, so before leaving for my train, I handed it to the realtor with a promise to call later with a decision. Back in the car, heading for the train station, Julie said, "Maybe this isn't God telling you this isn't the right place. I think you're just feeling pressure to make a decision you didn't expect to have to make today." She was right. This is a perfect example of how God can speak to us through another person.

While waiting for the train, we prayed for wisdom and clarity, acknowledging that if this was the place God wanted for me, He would keep it from being rented to someone else until I felt comfortable about making the commitment. Free from the pressure of having to decide immediately, I boarded the train, settled into my seat, and focused on the Lord. As the train rumbled along, peace returned to my heart and with it came joy. Within twenty minutes I was sure this was indeed the place God had prepared for me, and as I proceeded with the rental and the subsequent move, I never had another moment of doubt.

Once I made the decision, did God say, "You dummy! What was your problem? The place had everything you said you wanted." No, He just enveloped me in His love and peace. I felt as if He said, "Well done, Judy!" I had not made the decision based on outward circumstances but on the inner assurance that can only be found in His presence. Often we know immediately if something is right or not, but if we need time to be sure of His leading, God is patient. He won't snatch our answer to prayer out from under us. Sometimes when a thing seems too good to be true, it is. Other times, though, it is just God wanting to pour out His love on us.

The process I used to find a new home can be applied to any change we may be contemplating – new job, new church, or new group of friends. If we understand and believe that God has prepared a place for us and will show us the path and make a roadway, we're on our way. We stand on the truth of God's Word and listen for His voice. We activate our faith by speaking what we believe while guarding our tongue from speaking negative thoughts. Then we take steps in the direction we want to go. We stay tuned in to God, allowing His peace to rule in our hearts, even if it means a change in direction or a pause in the action. When we feel secure in God's peace, we can boldly go forward, assured we will end up in exactly the right place.

On the Way to New Things

As moving preparations continued, the weeks flew along. Starting each day in the presence of God, I had peace, joy, and a sense of being deeply, intimately loved under His care. People would ask me, sometimes with a sad, concerned face, "So how are you doing?"

I'd reply, "I'm doing great! God is so good. He is really taking care of me." I'm sure there were those who wondered about me, but it was true. I was living proof of Psalm 16:11. He had shown me the path of life through those Bible verses, and in His presence I was finding fullness of joy. Living close to Him brought *pleasures forevermore.*

In June I moved into my condo. My furniture was very much at home in its new surroundings. In July I took that trip to Colorado. The day I left, my next-door neighbors were moving out. The day I returned, I ran into a woman I had not seen before in the hall. She appeared to be about my age. "Hi," I said. "Are you my new neighbor?"

"Yes," she replied. "I'm Helene." After exchanging the customary glad-to-meet-yous, she asked, "Are you alone, too?"

"Yes, my husband passed away in March."

"Mine died in February," she said.

Further conversation revealed we had both moved from

distant smaller towns to be closer to our families, and we were both new to the area. We had gone through similar experiences with our husbands' illnesses. As we became better acquainted, we kept discovering more and more things in common. And more and more we came to appreciate what a blessing it is to have a treasured friend living right next door who likes to go shopping and go out for dinner once in a while and can relate to the challenges of adjusting to being singled out. We still marvel at the heavenly setup that put this together.

By August my *rivers in the desert* had sprung up as well. I visited several churches and soon found one where I'm blessed and can also be a blessing. I learned that the Bible college in Colorado where I had been taking online courses had a campus only thirty minutes from my home, and I enrolled there. The first time I visited, I found that one of the students was a woman who had been an online classmate two years earlier. She and I had met in person once while in the online class but lost touch after the class ended. Our reconnection blossomed into a wonderful friendship.

Each of our lives is like a jigsaw puzzle that will not be completed till the day we leave this earth. As one piece slips into place we can see where the next one is supposed to go. And as each part comes together, more of the big picture emerges. The secret to fulfillment is letting the Holy Spirit show us which piece goes next and where it fits. We are not given a box lid showing us what the completed picture will look like. I would never have chosen to live alone. I was very comfortable with married life, sharing joys and trials, decisions and responsibilities. When Alan was sick, I didn't expect him to die. But God was not caught off guard. He prepared my heart for what was to come, opened a way for me, and then led me where He wanted me to go.

With God in the driver's seat, my adjustment to living as

one person instead of half a couple became an adventure. Every day brought new opportunities to watch Him at work in my heart and in the hearts of those around me. My job was easy: *Trust in the LORD with all your heart, and lean not on your own understanding; in all your ways acknowledge Him, and He shall direct your paths* (Proverbs 3:5-6). I didn't need to know every detail about the road ahead because I had an intimate relationship with the Driver. It was enough for me that He knew the destination, and He was more than able to get us there.

This almost sounds like the end of the story, but the puzzle is nowhere near completion. The part that encompasses my life as Alan's wife is all in place. I can look at it and enjoy the picture, seeing the outline of each piece and how it fits together with the others. But my focus now is on all those pieces that are yet to be put together. Since I learned how to soak in God's presence, spiritual photosynthesis has been taking place in my heart. Knowledge and understanding I accumulated over the last forty years, filtered through my more recent comprehension of God's grace and unconditional love, are moving from my head to my heart. The Holy Spirit is continually bringing me new *wisdom and revelation in the knowledge of Him* (Ephesians 1:17). Even now, years later, I feel as if He and I are continually embarking on new adventures.

9

Thoughts, Words, and Deeds

Let the word of Christ dwell in you richly in all wisdom ... And whatever you do in word or deed, do all in the name of the Lord Jesus, giving thanks to God the Father through Him. Colossians 3:16-17

We hear a lot of talk about spiritual warfare, and the way it is often presented makes it sound very mysterious. However, most spiritual warfare takes place right in our minds. God has one idea, and the enemy wants us to go a different way. When we are in the middle of a battle, we may not even realize we are in one. It's easier to see the conflicts and their resolutions as we look back on our lives. Then we can see what they were and how we handled them.

While Alan was in the hospital, all of my energy went into being with him and trying to help him get well. I didn't know what kind of life we might be facing later with therapy, medications, and adjustments in our lifestyle. I certainly didn't expect the next phase to be easy, but I planned to face those situations when we got to that point. My focus was on the here and now.

When instead of getting well Alan went to be with Jesus, I faced a whole different future, one I had never contemplated. Immediately I found myself confronted with a big choice. At this most vulnerable time, it was very important to guard my thoughts. I didn't get to choose whether or not I would become a widow, but I did get to decide how I would respond to my circumstances and how I would go through this unexpected phase of life. I could go through it trusting God and believing His promises, or I could go through it the hard way. Fortunately, I had made the choice a week before Alan died, telling God that no matter what happened, I would trust Him. Everything I did in those early singled-out days was a reflection of that decision.

Losing a husband you really love, especially after being married for a very long time, is a shock. It is hard. I've been accused of making it look too easy. There was nothing easy about it. But I chose to trust God, be thankful, praise Him, and stay close to Him. Was I thankful because I had lost Alan? Of course not. But I was thankful, because God does promise never to leave me or forsake me. I was thankful for all the blessings Alan and I had enjoyed together and for family and friends who helped me through this time. I began my very first morning at home praising and worshiping the Lord. I'm convinced that this early choice paved the way for a smoother journey through the entire adjustment process.

Guarding Our Thoughts

In order to fight the good fight, we must guard our hearts and minds by deciding how we will think and what we will think about. Then we must stick to it. *As he* [a man] *thinks in his heart, so is he* (Proverbs 23:7). Thoughts continually come into our minds. They may come from God, from our own hearts, from the enemy, or from things we see and hear in our environment. Even if we are careful to guard what we watch and listen to, we don't have complete control over what thoughts come to us, but we do get to choose which ones get to stay. We are the gatekeepers. As Pastor Kenneth Hagin once said, "You can't keep a bird from landing on your head, but you don't need to let it make a nest in your hair."

Whenever I think about guarding my thoughts, I picture those TV ads for a mucus-clearing product. The cartoon depicts a living room with comfy, overstuffed chairs and sofas. Ugly, ill-mannered creatures are lounging on the sofas with their feet up, declaring they have just moved in and intend to stay. Mucus medicine comes to the rescue, and the interlopers are forced to leave. When negative thoughts try to worm their way into our minds, we must not entertain them; we must kick them out. The longer they stay, the more they will settle in, eventually moving into our hearts where they become attitudes, or strongholds. These are even harder to get rid of.

In 2 Corinthians 10:4-5 Paul tells us we have weapons to use against negative, unproductive thoughts. *For the weapons of our warfare are not carnal but mighty in God for pulling down strongholds, casting down arguments and every high thing that exalts itself against the knowledge of God, bringing every thought into captivity to the obedience of Christ.* I used to envision this process as somehow grabbing each stronghold, imagination, or thought by the scruff of the neck, dragging it to Jesus, and saying, "Okay, you evil thought, here you are. Now submit!" How tiring!

However, it is much simpler than that. If we read the verse carefully, whose obedience is Paul talking about? Christ's. Not our obedience *to* Christ but the obedience *of* Christ. And what do we know about His obedience? Philippians 2:8 says, *He humbled Himself and became obedient to the point of death, even the death of the cross.* When we encounter a thought that tries to exalt itself or make itself more real than the truth of

God's Word, we need to remind ourselves of what Jesus did for us. By refocusing on Jesus and His obedience in going to the cross, we flush out the negative thought.

For example, one Sunday not long ago, I was having lunch with a group of ladies from church. I told them about how on a recent trip I happened to be flying on the day the airline treated all the passengers to a free glass of champagne to celebrate the company's twentieth anniversary. One of the ladies questioned me. "How can you call yourself a Christian and be talking about drinking alcohol?" she asked, adding that apparently I must not be "sanctified."

For some reason, her remark hit a nerve, and my feelings were hurt. On the way home, instead of thinking about the good food and fun conversation we enjoyed or how special I had felt on the day the airline served the champagne, my mind kept going back to this one remark.

Who does she think she is, judging me? She's not so holy either! Maybe she would never touch champagne, but I'll bet she does plenty of other things Christians shouldn't do. Really mature thoughts, right? On it went, one negative thought rolling into the next. I had failed to guard my mind. A few more minutes and I'd have been wallowing in my old, familiar stronghold – self-pity – for the rest of the afternoon.

About halfway home I recognized the old thinking pattern. Knowing I had to bring those thoughts into captivity, I immediately chose to forgive this lady. Then I turned on joyful praise music to help me refocus my attention on the goodness of God. When I stopped mulling over the upsetting remark and began thanking God for His goodness and grace, my joy and peace returned. By the time I arrived home, I was free from self-pity, ready to enjoy the rest of my Sunday afternoon. I looked up the word *sanctified* and found that it means "set apart" with no mention of any particular behavior, and that made me feel even better.

Becoming Spiritually Minded

In Romans 8:1-11 Paul talks about being spiritually minded instead of carnally minded. We do this by renewing our minds through the Word of God, setting our minds on His promises, and lining up our thinking with them. Things of the flesh are what we perceive through our five senses (sight, hearing, touch, smell, and taste). Being carnally minded doesn't necessarily mean thinking sinful thoughts. It simply describes the condition of being focused on the flesh instead of the Spirit.

For to be carnally minded is death, but to be spiritually minded is life and peace (Romans 8:6). Our emotions are a God-given barometer to help us evaluate our thinking. Are we experiencing life and peace? This shows we are being spiritually minded. If not, our emotions indicate that we are letting our minds dwell more heavily on information from the five senses than on spiritual truth. A spiritually minded person says, "I don't care what the physical evidence looks like; I choose to stand on God's Word. That's what I believe."

Our emotions are a powerful force, and if we don't deal with the negative ones, they will influence our actions in a direction we don't really want to go. When the barometer says death instead of life and peace, we need to adjust our thinking. Many people are convinced you can't help how you feel, but we do *not* have to be victims of our emotions. Negative feelings are like negative thoughts in that we can't prevent them from coming, but we don't have to keep them. We can change how we feel by changing the way we think.

In addition to guarding our thoughts we must also be careful about the words we speak. There's a cute old saying, "Keep your words short and sweet, because you never know which ones you'll have to eat." In everyday conversation "eating your words" implies having said something wrong and now needing to admit it. This is not a pleasant experience. But according to the Bible, eating our words is even more serious than this, because we receive the results of what we say. "This won't work. Everything I do turns out badly." How many times have we all made such declarations? While this may not be how we want things to go, without our realizing it, we make statements that can have a negative impact on our lives and situations.

Why are spoken words so powerful? We find the answer in Genesis 1 where the writer describes the events of creation. Over and over in this chapter – nine times – we read, *God said ...* And every time God spoke, what He said came into being: light, continents, sky, oceans, plants, sun, moon, stars, animals, and finally the human race. He created man in His own image and in His likeness (Genesis 1:26-27). The creative force God used was the spoken word. Because He made us in His image and likeness our spoken words also have creative power.

Our Mighty Assault Weapon

In Ephesians 6:13-17 Paul lists the mighty spiritual weapons of our warfare. First he names five pieces of defensive armor: belt of truth, helmet of salvation, breastplate of righteousness, shoes of the gospel of peace, and shield of faith. Then he identifies our offensive assault weapon: the sword of the Spirit, which is the Word of God. And how do we activate this living, powerful sword? By speaking it. By finding a Scripture applicable to our situation and speaking those words over it, we release the power of the Holy Spirit into it.

Another Bible passage that clearly shows how our words affect our lives is Proverbs 18:20-21: *With the fruit of a man's mouth his stomach will be satisfied; he will be satisfied with the product of his lips. Death and life are in the power of the tongue, and those who love it will eat its fruit* (NASB). Three times these verses state we will indeed eat the results of what we say. The fruit of our mouth and the product of our lips are whatever comes from our mouth. Do we speak rotten, sour, or tasteless fruit? Or do we speak words of love, hope, and encouragement – even toward ourselves? This is what will feed us to satisfaction.

Death and life, according to this passage, are in the power of our tongue. Every time we say something negative we may not necessarily see an immediate, terrible result, but the cumulative effect of our words will eventually show up in our lives. We have the power to speak good things into our lives. This is not some New Age hocus-pocus. The words we speak must not only be positive, but in order to be empowered by the Holy Spirit, they must agree with God's written Word. Jesus said, *The words that I speak to you are Spirit, and they are life* (John 6:63). When our spoken words are the same as what God says, we set powerful spiritual forces in motion.

In addition to releasing life, speaking God's Word can actually release angels! Psalm 103:2 tells us, *Bless the Lord, O my soul*, and admonishes us to *forget not all His benefits* (NASB). The psalm continues by listing all of those benefits. But something different comes up in verse 20. Suddenly David is no longer speaking to his soul. He says, *Bless the Lord, you His angels, mighty in strength, who perform His word, obeying the voice of His word.* David is telling us that speaking God's Word sets His angels to work, causing them to perform on our behalf.

I had an experience with this recently when I found myself waiting for a number of business situations to be resolved, some of which affected other people besides me. I seemed to be getting nowhere when working with the bankers, tax people, and attorneys. Nothing was getting done the way it was supposed to be. I called to check on my long overdue tax return, and the CPA said my file was "in the stack." Another day I called my stepmother's attorney about a different tax matter and learned that the tax preparer had put our case "on the back burner" and then forgotten it. He promised to "put it back on the list." Nothing seemed to be getting done on time; I was beginning to see a very frustrating pattern.

The phrase "back burner" kept coming to my mind. "Lord," I prayed, "it seems as if I'm on everybody's back burner. Is there something I can do to get things going?" He reminded me of His promises in Deuteronomy 28 for all those who obey the Law. Of course, I couldn't obey the whole Law, but Jesus could and He did. He came to fulfill the Law (Matthew 5:17). Because of His death on the cross, all the blessings in Deuteronomy 28 now apply to everyone who believes on Him, so they applied to me. Verse 13 reads, *And the* LORD *will make you the head and not the tail; you shall be above only, and not be beneath.*

I began to wield my mighty sword, declaring the scripture from Deuteronomy and thanking God that according to His Word I was at the head, and not the tail, of the to-do lists; my files were above, on top of the stack, not buried somewhere beneath. Having recently learned that scripture about angels, I envisioned angels, *ministering spirits sent forth to minister for those who will inherit salvation* (Hebrews 1:14), putting my name on the tops of the to-do lists and moving my files to the tops of those piles. Within days every one of the business matters that had been in limbo for weeks was settled. Whether angels physically moved my files, I don't know. I do know that once I began proclaiming God's Word over my situation, things happened fast.

Before that, I had been expressing annoyance – and speaking death – by saying things like, "Nothing is happening, and there isn't anything I can do about it; I just have to wait." Yes, patience (long-suffering) is a fruit of the Spirit, but the problem in this case was not that I lacked patience. Something in the spiritual realm was hindering progress. Once I employed the sword of the Spirit, whatever had been blocking each item from being accomplished was removed, and the work was completed. Though I can't find any Scripture in the Bible giving us authority to command angels directly, it does say they will respond to *the voice of His Word*, and I most assuredly gave voice to His Word.

Actions Follow Our Heart

If our thoughts and words are lining up with Scripture, the arrow on our emotional barometer will point toward life and peace, and our actions will follow right along. We will find ourselves walking in the Spirit. *I say then: Walk in the Spirit, and you shall not fulfill the lust of the flesh* (Galatians 5:16). This is one of those verses we must read carefully, or we will misunderstand it. For years I got it backwards, reversing the cause and effect. I read it as, *God wants us to walk in the Spirit, so I must avoid fulfilling the lust (desires) of the flesh.* Not only is trying to get rid of the fleshly desires an exhausting process, but it puts the focus on our weaknesses and our efforts instead of on God's strength.

The verse really says that not fulfilling the desires of the flesh is a natural result or byproduct of walking in the Spirit. As we pursue our walk in the Spirit, we will find our desires changing with very little effort on our part. Picture a glass full of milk. If we place it under a running faucet, before long the milk will look more and more like water until eventually all of the milk will be replaced by water. We don't have to do anything to the milk. It just vanishes as we continue to pour in the water. This is what happens in our hearts as we renew our minds with the Word of God. As we allow the Holy Spirit to live through us and guide us, our fleshly desires will fade away. Could this be what Paul meant in Ephesians 5:26, when he talked about Jesus sanctifying His church *with the washing of water by the word*? Word in, junk out!

Walking in the Spirit means walking according to God's Word. This keeps our eyes on Jesus. Choosing to forgive instead of harboring resentment, as I did after that Sunday lunch, is an example of walking in the Spirit. Once I had decided to walk in the Spirit, turning my thoughts toward God and His goodness, the desire of my flesh (to be angry, to retaliate, to feel sorry for myself) melted away with no effort on my part. And once those desires were gone, I certainly wasn't in danger of fulfilling them.

A Heart for God

Our thoughts, words, and deeds are important, but the key to getting it right – having all of this lined up with God's Word – is being surrendered to His Spirit. For years I guarded my thoughts, watched my words, and did my best to obey the Word, but I had not completely given my heart to God. Then during the time Alan was in the hospital, I came to know Him in a different and more personal way. After that ten-week struggle, the one thing I cared most about didn't turn out the way I wanted. Alan died. Yet, I kept right on pursuing my walk with God. At the time I wasn't conscious of making a decision, but instead of pressing forward with God, I could have walked away from Him and gone back to doing things my own way.

Because I was already enjoying God's presence, the alternative never occurred to me. That commitment I made in the Family House – to trust God no matter what – gave me strength to accept the outcome, switch gears, and move forward. This is why I recommend not waiting till you're in a crisis situation to begin drawing closer to God. When a crisis comes, a person who is closely connected with God will automatically turn to Him. From my first day as a singled-out woman, I reveled in my intimacy with God. I continued listening for and following His voice. I knew Him well enough to know He is good and that it was not He who took Alan away from me. He does not steal, kill, and destroy.

Although God has shown me many things since then, I still don't have a clear understanding as to why Alan didn't receive a miraculous healing or at least make a gradual recovery. But I've always known the fault didn't lie with God. I'm convinced He wanted Alan healthy as much as I did. He gave us many opportunities in the earlier stages of Alan's illness to do things both physically and spiritually that could have changed the outcome, but we weren't listening. Now, although I knew my life had changed drastically, I also knew without a doubt I wouldn't be walking alone on this journey.

When I was a high school teacher, I knew a few colleagues who approached retirement grumbling and complaining about the school, their jobs, and their students. They could hardly wait to get out of the place. Their bitterness made the rest of us eagerly look forward to their getting out, too. Later, I would run into one of them out in the community and would ask, "How's retired life?" And guess what! They were still unhappy. On the other hand I had colleagues who enjoyed working right up till their last day. Yes, they were looking forward to the freedom of retirement, but they left happy. And as you may have surmised, they are also enjoying their retirement.

The point of this is that happiness is not based on our circumstances. It comes from an inner attitude. I loved Alan and our life together. We had great plans to move near our kids and enjoy growing old together. But when he was gone, I didn't "fall apart like a two-dollar suitcase." I kept walking with God. My life was not over. Yes, there were hard times and the singled-out life required many major adjustments, but I continued to be a happy person, not because of widowhood, but in spite of it. I just find the goodness of God so overwhelming I can't begin to express it adequately.

Every day brings opportunities to think, speak, and act according to God's Word. Thinking according to His Word brings life and peace. The Holy Spirit, who leads us into all truth and teaches us all things, empowers us to choose life and peace (John 16:13; 14:26). If we are becoming spiritually minded, our thoughts will line up with the Scriptures and pull our emotions into line. Jesus said, *Out of the abundance of the heart the mouth speaks* (Matthew 12:34). As the truths of the Bible abundantly fill our hearts, we will pour forth words of encouragement, faith, and hope. We will be blessed every time we eat our words.

As we choose to walk in the Spirit, we will find ourselves becoming less prone to fulfilling the desires of the flesh. Instead of anger, depression, discouragement, and bitterness, the fruit of the Spirit (love, joy, peace, patience, kindness, goodness, faithfulness, gentleness, and self-control) described in Galatians 5:22-23 will be apparent in our lifestyles, activities, and relationships. When we commit ourselves to walking intimately with God, He will respond. He is more eager for intimacy than we are to seek it. *Draw near to God and He will draw near to you* (James 4:8). It has been said that ninety percent of spiritual warfare is fought between our ears. So let's go for it! Let's renew our minds, speak life, walk in the Spirit, and win those battles.

10

Enjoying God's Presence

He who dwells in the secret place of the Most High
shall abide under the shadow of the Almighty.
Psalm 91:1

Reflecting on my forty-plus years of walking with God, I'm amazed I never realized what was lacking in my relationship with Him. If I had taken the trouble to ask what was missing, the answer would have been obvious. If I had looked back upon those times when I felt closest to Him and experienced the most peace and looked for the common denominator, it would have been easy to spot. I think of how disappointed Jesus was in His disciples when they were afraid of the storm and amazed to see Him calm the sea and walk on the water. The Bible says they *considered not the miracle of the loaves: for their heart was hardened* (Mark 6:52 KJV). We need to look back on our lives and consider those times when God was very real and present in our lives and understand why we experienced Him that way.

As a brand-new believer, overwhelmed by His peace and love, I would go on walks, quietly singing and having conversations with God. I could hardly wait for the opportunity to get out there! Then life crowded in and those times became fewer and less frequent until gradually they stopped happening. Years later, as a commuter, I would sometimes use my forty-minute train ride to tune out the world and bask in His presence (learning the hard way that I had to keep my eyes open and watch for my station). Usually I would emerge from those times fresh, energized, and full of peace. Yet, they were not regular occurrences. I would generally use the time to grade papers or chat with other passengers. After I retired, during the summer before we sold our home, I spent delicious moments with God while Alan was sleeping and I was resting. Yet, even those times slipped away when I got busy with other things.

Now that I understand the problem, I'm mystified as to why the connection between time alone with God and the peace that passes understanding sailed right over my head through those years. The difference between all those previous times of closeness and the intimacy that developed while I was staying at the Family House was a matter of desire and commitment. Those earlier encounters with God were somewhat serendipitous. I had some free time and chose to spend it with God. While I enjoyed it at the time, I never made it a priority. At the Family House, I deliberately set aside time to listen to God. This is similar to the difference between giving sporadically when you have extra money as opposed to consistent, deliberate tithing.

The first few days as I sat with *Jesus Calling*, I spent only a few minutes each day. This doesn't mean once I put the book down and headed for the hospital, my prayer time was over and I left God sitting there. I tried to *pray without ceasing*, looking for moments to get alone with God throughout the day. But there was a new determination in my heart about that private time first thing in the morning. For those few minutes, I focused all my attention on what God was saying to me through the devotional. Peace would settle on my heart. Then I would get up and go out to face the world.

Then came the day I committed to a half hour each day. I came to these morning sessions with a new attitude. First, I determined to be there every day for a set amount of time. Second, I had a desire to hear from God, a hunger to feel and experience His presence. I wasn't asking Him for anything; I just wanted to be with Him. My only commitment was to be there every morning and to be listening. And that was all He had been waiting for. How awesome it is to touch hearts with God at unexpected moments, but with all the distractions in daily life, those encounters are certainly not as frequent as He would like from us.

Psalm 37:3-4 says, *Trust in the LORD and do good; dwell in the land and cultivate faithfulness. Delight yourself in the LORD; and He will give you the desires of your heart* (NASB). This scripture, a long-time favorite, finally made it from my head to my heart during that time. As I cultivated faithfulness by being there in that chair every morning, God did speak to me. My trust in Him began to grow. This is evident in the nightly e-mails I was sending out. As I began to delight in His presence, He placed a strong desire in my heart to know Him better. Then He fulfilled that desire by becoming more real to me. Jeremiah 29:13 says, *And you will seek Me and find Me, when you search for Me with all your heart.* I can see now that I had never done that before, not really.

Hanging Out with God

After returning home, I enjoyed those morning times even more. For one thing, on most days I had no need to run off, so I could spend more than half an hour if I wanted. I also had my stereo and all my praise and worship CDs. Recently I mentioned to someone how much I enjoy just hanging out with God, not asking Him for anything. She asked, "But what do you do for all that time?" Realizing she is probably not the only one who might wonder about that, I will share some of the ways I spend my time with God. Just like when you spend time with any friend, every day is not the same. There are lots of things He and I enjoy doing together.

I most definitely do *not* use this time to bring a shopping list of things I want God to do for me. Sometimes I just sit and listen. I command my mind and emotions, "Peace, be still," and just wait to hear God speak to me. If goofy, unproductive thoughts keep coming in and bouncing around like those ugly creatures in the mucus medicine commercial, I switch to a different activity. On days I'm able to be quiet, God may bring to mind a Bible verse, something I've heard in a sermon or read in a book, or a new way of looking at a situation I have been thinking about. Or He may reveal connections between two different passages or between a Bible passage and circumstances I'm dealing with – spiritual photosynthesis.

Another day I may use the time to proceed with my journey through the Bible, as I described in an earlier chapter. I find it useful to read out loud for two reasons. First, it helps me stay focused. I can't tell you how many times I've read an entire chapter silently and then realized I had no idea what I just read. This is less apt to happen when I read aloud. The second reason is that since *faith comes by hearing, and hearing by the word of God,* speaking the Word aloud brings it to our ear, building faith (Romans 10:17). If you aren't alone in your house, you can whisper. As long as you can hear it, faith will come. When a verse or passage suddenly comes alive, I talk to God about it, almost as if I were explaining it to a friend. If I come to something I don't understand, I ask Him about it. The answer may not come right then, but I trust Him to explain it to me eventually.

Music plays a big part, too, in my so-called quiet time. There are mornings where I spend the entire half hour singing along, maybe even dancing, with my praise and worship music. I've made playlists of quiet songs, lively songs, and just plain good songs, and I weeded out songs that beg and plead with God or do not line up with Scripture. Because death and life are in the power of the tongue, I want to sing words that will speak life into my heart (Proverbs 18:21). If I'm having a hard time keeping my eyes on Jesus, I go for my praise and thanks playlist in which every song reminds me of the goodness of God and helps me proclaim it. At these times it's good to sing with a loud voice. The enemy hates that!

Meditating on a verse or passage from the Bible is a very productive use of the time. Think of a cow chewing her cud, working it over and over, digesting and redigesting. Going over and over a verse, word by word, really brings those words to life, painting a picture in my mind. I always thought meditating was a mental process, mulling over ideas or pictures silently, until I learned one of the definitions of the word *meditate* is "to mutter or to speak." Once again, speaking the truth helps establish it in our hearts.

Many people start their quiet time with a devotional. There are many wonderful devotional books out there, some general and others more topical. You can also find daily devotionals online, which can be delivered to your e-mail, and most of these are free. It isn't necessary to spend the entire time doing the same thing. For my first year, I started each day with *Jesus Calling*, then went into another activity. I keep talking about the half hour, but there is nothing magical about the amount of time. I suggest you decide upon a length of time that is doable for you, then commit to staying there for that amount of time, just as I did for a half hour at the Family House. Otherwise, when you show up to meet with God and nothing seems to be happening, it may be tempting to just get up and go do something else. Consistency – cultivating faithfulness – is extremely important.

What Good Is It?

Something else I do frequently may be unfamiliar to you: praying and singing in the Spirit, also known as speaking in tongues. For this you use a language which the Lord gives through the baptism in the Holy Spirit as described in Acts 2:1-4. You'll find several resources that explain more about this at the back of the book. I realize there is some controversy about this spiritual gift among traditional, denominational Christians in the United States, but many believers around the world accept it as a normal part of the Christian walk, just as they accept other truths in the Bible. In my case, the baptism in the Holy Spirit is not only an important part of my Christian walk, but it was because of the gift of speaking in tongues that I became a Christian when I did. Let me explain.

Alan and I had been married ten years but not very happily. Everyone around us could see we were having problems. One evening my neighbor Elaine invited me out for dessert at a local café. I knew she was a Christian, so I expected her to bombard me with marital advice or lecture me about my sinful ways. Instead, as we lingered over coffee, she informed me that she and several other neighbors had recently received the baptism in the Holy Spirit and were speaking in tongues.

Though I didn't have a personal relationship with Jesus at that time, I did attend a church and had read the Bible. I knew the apostles spoke in tongues on the day of Pentecost in the book of Acts. But that was in Jerusalem back in Bible times. This was Mission, Kansas, in 1972. It all sounded pretty far-fetched to me, and I said as much to Elaine. Then I said, "I guess it's fine for you guys, but what good is it?"

She explained that when you pray in tongues, the Holy Spirit gives the words, so although you don't understand what you're saying, you know you're praying according to God's will. You're praying exactly the right thing because you're not depending on your own mind (Romans 8:26). "Hmph," I replied and quickly changed the subject. I couldn't have shown less interest. Elaine also told me the neighbors were praying for me and for my marriage. I didn't appreciate this; I'd already been to see a lawyer about starting divorce proceedings.

Elaine told me later that after she got home, she went to God in tears saying, "I'm so sorry, Lord. I thought You wanted me to share this with Judy. I guess I must have misunderstood You. Please forgive me for casting my pearls before swine." When I got home, I tried to get what Elaine had just told me out of my mind. However, unknown to her, what she had said about all these neighbors going around praying perfect prayers, aligned with God's will, intrigued me. I simply couldn't get that thought out of my mind. It would pop up unexpectedly and uninvited while I was washing dishes, driving the car, buying groceries. The Holy Spirit kept reminding me of Elaine's words, creating a longing in my heart that my mind wasn't aware of.

My life and marriage were in a mess, but I was afraid to pray. I'd heard people say, "Be careful what you pray for. You just might get it," and that really scared me. I was afraid I might pray for something that would make things even worse, and God would answer that prayer. I wanted His help but had no idea what I wanted Him to do. I just knew I wasn't happy. Money problems had dogged us since the beginning of our marriage and had escalated over the years. Our inability to get on top of our finances led to many disagreements and resentments. We were immature going into the marriage, and ten years and two children later we still hadn't learned to function as a unit, financially or in any other way. No wonder the thought of being able to pray for the right things appealed to me.

Then one day I came home from work to find a note from the babysitter taped to my door. "The kids and I are all at Elaine's. Come on over."

Uh-oh, I thought. *They're having one of those prayer meetings. They're probably going to try to get me to talk in tongues. Oh well, I'll just pretend to go along with it, and when they see I can't do it, they'll leave me alone.* I walked in to find about a dozen people sitting in a circle on the floor. They said God had told them I would receive the baptism in the Holy Spirit that day.

"That's nice," I said, with little enthusiasm, attributing this pronouncement to wishful thinking on their part rather than a word from God.

Elaine asked if I would like to receive a prayer language. "Oh," I answered in my most humble, pious voice. "I'm not worthy."

"Well, praise God," she replied. "I'm glad you realize that. No one is worthy!" *Oops, that one didn't work!*

She asked me again and I shrugged my shoulders. The group prayed together in tongues to let me see what it was like. I don't know what I expected, but I liked hearing their prayer. Each person's language was different from the others, and the sound of their combined voices was soothing. It was calm and orderly, not in the least bit weird or uncontrolled as I had imagined it might be. When she asked the third time, I realized I really did want to be able to pray without being afraid of asking for the wrong things. So, I answered, "I guess so."

Elaine explained that before Jesus could baptize me in the Holy Spirit, I would need to belong to Him. She asked if I was willing to confess my sins to God, invite Jesus into my heart, and let Him run my life. I readily agreed. It was obvious I hadn't done a very good job of running it myself, so I had nothing to lose. After Elaine led me in a prayer to receive Jesus, everyone hugged me and welcomed me into God's family. We sat back down, and she led me in a second prayer asking Jesus to baptize me in the Holy Spirit. Within minutes I was speaking in tongues. Although not everyone who prays for the baptism in the Holy Spirit begins speaking in tongues immediately, I did.

As I prayed in my new language along with the group, I felt a surge of God's love and peace go through me. The rest of that day and evening I moved around as if blanketed in a warm fog, feeling truly secure for the first time in years. When I went to bed that night, I opened my Bible and started reading. I'd read the whole New Testament through many times, but this time words and phrases I didn't remember ever reading before stuck out like boldface print.

I eventually learned that praying in the Spirit has more benefits for us than helping us pray according to God's will. It also edifies us or builds us up spiritually and keeps us in the love of God (1 Corinthians 14:4; Jude 1:20-21). As we speak in tongues, we speak mysteries and hidden wisdom (1 Corinthians 14:2; 2:6-7). When I pray in the Spirit, I ask God for an interpretation of the mysteries and wisdom I am speaking. Many times as I continue to pray, the answer to a problem I've been asking about will suddenly become clear.

One of my favorite benefits of praying in the Spirit is described in Isaiah 28:11-12: *For with stammering lips and another tongue He will speak to this people, to whom He said, "This is the rest with which you may cause the weary to rest," and, "this is the refreshing."* That makes me think of lying down to rest in green pastures beside still waters. That's why it's an important part of my time with God.

In the days, weeks, and months to follow, despite being able to pray perfect prayers, I still made many mistakes, but God began the process of transforming my heart. Some attitudes changed right away. I no longer wanted a divorce. I really wanted to be a good wife and mother. The Holy Spirit was at work in my life. In fact, my attitude and behavior toward Alan changed so drastically that within a few months, he gave his life to Jesus as well, and a few weeks later he received the baptism in the Holy Spirit.

Easy Way or Hard Way?

I've shared this story to let you know Jesus is still baptizing believers in the Holy Spirit today, just as He did two thousand years ago on the day of Pentecost. I believe my Christian walk would have been much more arduous without this. I'm not saying it can't be done, because there are certainly people who are much closer to God than I am, even though they don't speak in tongues. But when I think about trying to follow Christ and live according to the Bible without the added help of the spiritual gifts, I remember something that happened many years ago when Alan's elderly aunt came to live with us. After dinner the first night, wanting to be helpful, she filled up the sink with sudsy water and washed the dishes for us. For several weeks we let her do this, not mentioning that we had a dishwasher. We thought washing the dishes made her feel important and more at home.

Then one day as she sat at the table with her coffee, she looked over toward our portable dishwasher and pointed to it. "What's that box for?" she asked.

We showed her the inside and explained how it worked.

"You mean we can just put the dirty dishes in that thing and it can wash and dry 'em all for us?"

Yes, we nodded.

"Then what have we been doing all this work for?" Thus ended Aunt Ruth's dishwashing career!

When Alan explained we thought she liked washing them by hand, she looked at him as if he'd just said the craziest thing she had ever heard. The point is, when there's a tool available to make the job easier, why not use it?

Having been baptized in the Holy Spirit on the same day I received my salvation, I can't compare my walk with God before and after. I don't know which changes in my life were due to being born again and which were a result of the baptism in the Holy Spirit. Nevertheless, others who talk about their before-and-after differences describe a richer, fuller, more powerful Christian walk afterwards. One friend told me she'd been a Christian for more than twenty years but never experienced God's overwhelming love and power in her life until she received the baptism in the Holy Spirit and began speaking in tongues. The baptism in the Holy Spirit doesn't make me a better Christian than someone who hasn't received it, but it most assuredly makes me a better Christian than I would have been without it.

Jesus said that one of the signs that would follow those who believed would be speaking in tongues (Mark 16:17-18). Before ascending into heaven, He instructed His disciples not to leave Jerusalem until they were baptized in the Holy Spirit, which would clothe them with power from on high (Acts 1:4-8). If the apostles and disciples, who walked with Jesus in person for over three years and spent time with Him after he was raised from the dead, needed this extra boost of power, I think we probably do, too. I'm certainly glad to have a prayer language for those times I really don't know how to pray for a situation, and singing in the Spirit enhances my times with God.

I remember a time when Alan and I were reading Psalm 91. The first verse says, *He who dwells in the secret place of the Most High shall abide under the shadow of the Almighty.* As we read, we were looking at a watercolor on our wall, painted by a friend, showing a group of sheep standing under the shade of a tree. The artist had told us the painting was inspired by that verse. I told Alan, "I want to know what that means. Where is that secret place?" We decided that would be a good thing to find out, but we didn't pursue it at the time.

Now I understand that it is the place of intimacy where we are alone with God. In order to abide under the shadow of the Almighty, we need to *dwell* in the intimacy, not just visit occasionally. For me, one way of doing that is praying or singing in tongues, speaking a language known only to God. How could anything be more secret or more intimate? No wonder the apostle Paul said, *I thank my God I speak with tongues more than you all*, and *I wish you all spoke with tongues* (1 Corinthians 14:18; 14:5).

You may never have heard about speaking in tongues, or you may have been told that the Bible teaches against it. I think some of the controversy may be due to a misunderstanding of Paul's instructions to the church in Corinth. In 1 Corinthians 12, 13, and 14 Paul was correcting the believers not because they were speaking in tongues, but becaue they were misusing the gift. Their church services were disorderly, and he corrected several of their other practices as well. In 1 Corinthians 13:1 he warned that speaking in tongues, if not used in love, is just noise, and he wrote an entire chapter defining and describing the love in which all the spiritual gifts should be used. He was exhorting the believers to use tongues in an orderly manner

Paul did not advocate they stop because the gift was being misused, any more than we would advise people to stop using electricity because misuse of it can harm or kill people. In fact, he ended the whole discourse on spiritual gifts by saying, *Therefore, brethren, desire earnestly to prophesy, and do not forbid to speak with tongues. Let all things be done decently and in order* (1 Corinthians 14:39-40). If you have questions about this topic, I would strongly recommend that you read all of 1

Corinthians 12, 13 and 14 in context, and avail yourself of the materials listed in the Resources section of this book.

Speaking in tongues is a beautiful gift and a special tool that helps me in my walk with God. However, it is also very obvious from the rest of my story that being baptized in the Holy Spirit and speaking in tongues is no guarantee of intimacy with God. It is certainly no substitute for meditating on the Scriptures, making the truth our own, and spending time with God so spiritual photosynthesis can take place in our heart. I was connected to this amazing power source all those years, but I had never turned the dimmer switch all the way up!

Time to Draw Close

Regardless of what you believe about speaking in tongues, I hope this book is encouraging you to seek intimacy with God now and pursue spiritual mindedness before trouble comes. I certainly wish I had done it sooner. However, you may already be in the middle of a trial. If so, don't despair. It's never too late to pursue a rich, meaningful relationship with Him. *Draw near to God and He will draw near to you* (James 4:8). Your circumstances may be overwhelming – mine certainly were. But as you earnestly seek Him, God will come along beside you and strengthen you right in the middle of the trial.

What a beautiful promise we find in Isaiah 43:1-3: *Fear not, for I have redeemed you; I have called you by your name; you are Mine. When you pass through the waters, I will be with you; and through the rivers, they shall not overflow you. When you walk through the fire, you shall not be burned, nor shall the flame scorch you, for I am the LORD your God.* Isn't that awesome? He knows your name. You are His.

Make the commitment to set aside some time and seek God deliberately and consistently. He longs for this deep, meaningful relationship with us. He is more interested in being with us than in what we can do for Him. We need to have this same attitude toward Him. We need to want Him more than we want what He can do for us. This is so simple, yet I just didn't get it for over four decades. Just think – the Almighty God, Creator of the universe, who holds the worlds in His hand, wants to hang out with you! Invitations abound in His Word. What are you waiting for?

11

New Things Springing Forth

For I know the plans I have for you," declares the
Lord, "plans to prosper you and not to harm you,
plans to give you hope and a future.
Jeremiah 29:11 (NIV)

As I write this chapter, I've been singled out for just a little
over two years. When I contemplated my future the
week after Alan died, and God showed me those passages in
Isaiah 42 and 43 about breaking from the past and expecting
new things, I couldn't begin to imagine what my new journey
would be like or where it would take me. Looking back, I see that
God has been fulfilling everything He promised, right before
my eyes, beginning with taking me by the hand (Isaiah 42:6).
Even now, when I close my eyes, I can picture myself walking
hand in hand with Jesus on a path.

In Isaiah 42:9 and 43:18 He instructed me to break with the
past. Of course, if I completely forgot the past, I wouldn't have
been able to write this book! But God simply meant He didn't
want me tied to the past – the sadness of my loss, the old ways
of thinking, the fear that once held me back.

Knowing I would be relocating made letting go of the past easier than it might have been if I had continued living in our house. Right after the funeral, I started the clearing-out process, which forced me to think about my future. I involved myself in church activities, too, which took the focus off me. Any time I recognized thoughts of loneliness or self-pity trying to creep into my thinking, I would speak to them and throw them out, deliberately making myself think about moving preparations or the next activity on the calendar.

Occasionally a zinger would catch me unaware. For example, one day as I was getting my nails done, a married couple walked into the salon wanting pedicures. As they settled into adjoining chairs and plunged their feet into the tubs of swirling water, they told everyone this was part of their thirty-eighth anniversary celebration. I started to say, "My husband and I have been married fifty-one years," when suddenly reality hit me in my chest like a sledgehammer. I'm sure my manicurist wondered why I was blinking back tears as she worked on my nails (she wasn't doing that bad of a job).

Another day I was cleaning out Alan's dresser drawers. I had made it just fine through his socks, ties, handkerchiefs, and underwear, and then I opened the undershirt drawer. Those clean-smelling, neatly folded T-shirts, waiting in readiness for their old friend who would never be there to take them out and wear them, caused me to dissolve into tears. So I hugged the T-shirts, breathed in the Alan smell, and had a good cry. Then I put them back into the drawer, closed it, and walked away to find a different task to work on. I experienced enough of these unbidden reminders "out of the blue" without purposely lingering in the past. I had to let it go.

God promised new things to come (Isaiah 42:9; 43:19). My life is full to overflowing with new things that seem to be simply springing into existence. Travel is one example. During our years together, Alan and I did very little traveling. In the earlier years we simply couldn't afford it. Then his work required him to travel, and the last thing he wanted to do when he could schedule vacation time was turn around and take off on a trip. Once he left the job that required traveling, he had come to hate flying. He said he would never get on another airplane unless it was absolutely necessary. Our last trip by air had been in 1996 for a funeral in Florida. Long car trips were problematic too, because he didn't want to leave the house unattended for too many days at a time.

When I found myself alone, I realized there was no reason to continue being a homebody. My first trip beyond Illinois was the one to Colorado that I had planned with my sister. I discovered I enjoy flying. I even like airports, considering them part of the whole adventure. (I'm easily amused.) Over the next two years, I flew twelve more times, and I continue to enjoy air travel.

I've also taken many auto trips. The first one was a five-hour drive to northern Wisconsin. No more fear of driving! It quickly became obvious that the minivan Alan enjoyed so much was way more car than I needed – or could handle, especially in my parking garage. I had scratches on the bumpers to prove it. So, I traded it in for a brand new SUV, the first car I ever personally owned. New condo, new car, new freedom to travel; yes, God was definitely doing new things!

My *rivers in the desert*, the church and Bible college classes that God led me to, turned out to be just right for me also. Paul instructed Timothy, *Be diligent* [study] *to present yourself approved to God as a workman who does not need to be ashamed, accurately handling the word of truth* (2 Timothy 2:15 NASB). The things I've learned at Bible college have taught me how important it is to understand the whole Word of God and to look at individual verses and passages from the context of the entire Bible. I'm learning to *rightly divide the word of truth.* Bible college has helped me deepen my relationship with God and get to know Him better. Daily, I'm learning how to share these truths with others.

New friends? Wow! Not only did God put one right next door, but shortly after I started attending the church, I became acquainted with Mary, another recently singled-out woman. We went to lunch together one day. The next week we invited two more ladies to join us. Before long, Mary had accumulated a whole group of women, and we started going out to lunch every Sunday after church. Between church and Bible college, God supplied me with many friends.

Playing the cello was the biggest surprise of all. I have the piano my parents bought when I was seven, and I plink around on it once in a while but have never mastered it. One day I was telling a friend I wished I could play it but lacked the coordination to get all those fingers to do different things. She suggested I try an instrument where you play only one note at a time. Somehow we came upon the idea of the cello. "Okay, Lord," I said. "I'm not sure whether I want to do this or not." It was certainly nothing I had ever thought of doing. "But if this idea is from You, then please help me get lined up with a teacher without having to make a career out of looking for one."

Within a couple hours, after only three phone calls, I had found a cello teacher right in my town who, it turns out, really enjoys working with adult students, even uncoordinated ones. I rented an instrument and we were off and running. I must say that even though you only play one note at a time, playing the cello is not easy. Coordination is still an issue. I'd like to say that I just started out with no problems, sounding like Yo-Yo Ma from the very first lesson. I'd be lying, of course. It was a struggle learning how to hold the bow, which finger goes with which note, and even how to hold the cello. After two years I still haven't removed the tapes showing me where to put my fingers.

After about six months, I played in my first recital. I was not pleased with my performance. My son, daughter, and four of the grandchildren were there, and I think they were embarrassed for me, although they never said so. I came very close to quitting then. When I brought up the subject with God, He said, "If you want to stop, you can; but do you really want to go out in defeat?" So I stuck with it.

Then after about a year of lessons and one much better recital, I was invited to join the worship team at church. I found the worship music much easier to play than the pieces for my lessons – longer, sustained notes instead of tricky bowing and fast passages. The cello really sounds good with all the voices and other instruments, which is highly motivating, and I enjoy being part of the team. Worship is a very important part of my relationship with God, so helping to lead the congregation into His presence is a joyous highlight in my week. No one seems to care that I'm not perfect. I'm continuing with the lessons, because some day I hope to be able to play really well.

Travels, Bible college, and the cello are just the beginning of all the new things God has lined up for me. In addition to promising new things, He had spelled out the purpose He was calling me to: *to open blind eyes, to bring out prisoners from the dungeon and those who dwell in darkness from the prison* (Isaiah 42:7). As for opening blind eyes and freeing the prisoners, God made it very clear He was not talking about physical blindness or prisons. My calling was to help those precious people in His body who are blinded by not knowing who they are in Him, and trapped by their wrong thinking. How was I going to do that? I shared the passages from Isaiah with my pastor, as well as God's explanation to me. He suggested I participate in Bible studies at the church and look for opportunities to share my understandings with people in those settings. He seemed very happy to have me on board.

Shortly after moving, I decided to join the writers' group my daughter belonged to, although she was not currently involved in it. I had attended with her a few times several years earlier when Alan and I were visiting her, and I thought it would be an interesting way to spend two evenings a month. At my first meeting the other members suggested I try writing a couple devotionals for a book they were putting together so they could get an idea of my writing style. I did, and the response was encouraging. I enjoyed writing the devotionals. They provided opportunities to share little tidbits of wisdom God had given me. Next thing you know, I was thinking about writing a book.

As I learn more about God's Word. I realize that I have sometimes misunderstood a verse or passage, such as the one in Galatians 5:16 about walking in the Spirit so as not to fulfill the lust of the flesh, which I mentioned earlier. And other times I have inadvertently taken verses out of context, leading to wrong thinking. As I continue to discover these insights, my various writing and speaking activities will provide opportunities to share them with other believers. I think this is what God meant when He said He wanted me to help other believers understand the Word. When we are misunderstanding what God is telling us, we're not able to walk in the freedom He wants us to enjoy.

Hopefully, this book is already opening some spiritual eyes. While I don't know how this book is helping you, my hope is that it's helping you understand some truths you may not have seen before, and that you will be encouraged as you see who the Lord is, and what He has for You as His child. God has definitely brought exciting new things into my life, just as He promised, so I'm sure He will show me how to do the rest of what He has called me to when the time is right. He is faithful.

I was fine with God holding me by the hand; I had no problem with forgetting the past and I was enjoying the new things God was doing. I knew that in His time and way He would fulfill the rest of that passage in my life. But then God began speaking to me about a little statement almost hidden in the middle of the Isaiah 42 passage: *and I will not give My glory to another, Nor My praise to graven images* (v. 8). I had skipped over this, not ignoring it exactly, but not really giving it much attention, because it didn't seem to fit right there in the middle of "my" scripture. What did that have to do with me, and new things, and opening blind eyes, and freeing prisoners? When we come to something that doesn't seem to make sense, it's a good idea to ask God to show us how it applies to us, so I did.

Then one day, bingo! I saw it. Once upon a time Lucifer had been God's heavenly worship leader, His anointed cherub. God had gifted him magnificently, even given him built-in musical instruments. But this was not enough for Lucifer. He wanted God's glory; he wanted to become the object of angelic worship. He ended up losing his heavenly position and anointing because, although God is gracious and gives us everything He has, He will not share His glory. That belongs to Him alone. (You can read the whole story in Ezekiel 28:1-19.)

"Father," I asked after contemplating about Lucifer for a while, "are there areas in my life where I've been trying to steal Your glory? Please reveal them to me, so I can stop doing that and give the glory back to You." God had been working with me for a while in the area of money. Now I began to see that although I had been giving with the right motives, I had done some of it in a way that caused the recipients to look upon me, instead of Him, as their source of supply. I quickly repented and asked Him to show me how to turn this around.

He showed me that whether the currency we are giving to others is tangible like money or other material goods or something less tangible such as time, counsel, or help with a problem, the principle is the same. We should be motivated by the desire to be a blessing and advance the kingdom of God. But if the person or ministry views us as the solution to their problem instead of trusting their Jehovah-Jireh Provider God, the glory is going to us. It's a very awesome feeling to know God has used us to answer another person's prayer, but we must always be careful to give the glory right back to God. Our response to their thanks must always be, "God put it on my heart to do (or say, or give) it. Isn't He good?"

While I was not deep in the throes of glomming up all of God's glory for myself, there were a few situations where I had come close or unintentionally could have done so. He reminded me of one particular commitment I had made without consulting Him first, and although things turned out well for all concerned, there had been a better plan and I had gotten in the way. This gentle warning set me back on the right path and opened my spiritual eyes to a greater understanding of kingdom principles.

Solomon wrote, *Like apples of gold in setting of silver is a word* [fitly] *spoken in right circumstances* (Proverbs 25:11 NASB). Wouldn't that make a beautiful piece of jewelry? And when God Himself speaks a fitly spoken word to us, how precious it is – beyond the most gorgeous piece of jewelry imaginable. That was how I felt when He revealed the connection between my activities and the Isaiah 42:8 verse about His glory.

My life is quickly filling up with good things, as promised in Psalm 103:5. God is revealing my gifts and strengths, bringing them to light in new ways. He is providing opportunities for me to share these gifts to bless others and advance His kingdom. He is opening doors almost faster than I can walk through them. But He loves me too much to let me take His glory upon myself. He wants me to walk in the Spirit, at His direction, and by His power. He doesn't want me to let my flesh get in the way or to think His accomplishments are my own.

Yes, this word was fitly spoken, its significance revealed to me at the right time, in the right circumstances. This golden apple of wisdom had been there all the time, nestled in the center of timely silver passages about making peace with the past, facing the future, and knowing my calling. God's timing is perfect. I had done enough right things and wrong things for Him to be able to show me the differences and bring me to a new level of intimacy. He used the area of money as a teaching tool, but the principle of giving Him the glory applies to every area of our lives. He gently led me to this understanding before I got to thinking I was pretty awesome.

As with all of God's principles, there is a balance. We do need to know our true identity in Him. In Him we *are* awesome. However, in the flesh, we cannot please God (Romans 8:8). Pride caused our enemy's downfall. Wouldn't he just love to see us make the same mistake! But God is gracious. He wants to bless us. That's why He calls us to draw near to Him. He wants us to bask in His love, rest in His peace, carry His joy to the world, and give Him all the glory.

All of the new things God brought into my life kept me very active, but not too busy to spend time with Him. One scripture kept coming to mind to describe my situation: *The lines have fallen to me in pleasant places* (Psalm 16:6). Everywhere I looked, I saw people and events falling into place for me. Yes, I missed Alan, but my journey with God was an exciting adventure. Even as I reveled in His goodness, I couldn't possibly have imagined the next new thing He had lined up for me.

12

God Is Not Anonymous

And we know that all things work together for good to those who love God, to those who are the called according to His purpose. Romans 8:28

Contemplating the events of my life so far makes my head spin. Many of them occurred in an easily observed linear sequence. For example, God promised to *make a road in the wilderness and rivers in the desert* (Isaiah 43:19). I came to the Chicago area to find a new place to live, and He led the way through the wilderness of a constantly changing rental market to my ideal home. Once relocated, I found rivers – places of spiritual refreshment. Everything fell into place very neatly, a step at a time.

In other situations, however, things didn't appear to be falling into place. Our lives are like beautiful tapestries. We only see what is happening on the surface, but God is always at work behind the scenes, crossing threads and tying knots. Eventually the complete picture emerges and we realize God was at work the whole time. Sometimes we are privileged to hear about other stories that were intertwined with ours, and when we realize how intricately the situations and events all fit together, we can't help but marvel at God's mind-blowing love, grace, and mercy.

Albert Einstein once said, "Coincidences are God's way of choosing to remain anonymous." While I agree with him that God is involved in every so-called coincidence, I don't believe He intends to remain anonymous. He has a plan for each of our lives, many interwoven plans, and He leaves His fingerprints all over them. Let me show you what I mean.

God began preparing a beautiful tapestry just before Thanksgiving in 2011, but in order to show you the amazing artistry, we need to take a brief trip back to 2004. I shared in an earlier chapter how God spoke to me when Alan and I decided to sell our house in the North Shore suburbs of Chicago, telling me not to set our sights too low, giving us confidence to ask more for the house than we had originally planned. The next day we sold it for a price that was exceedingly, abundantly above all of our expectations.

God had rescued us from our paycheck-to-paycheck existence. After we paid off our mortgage, He led us to move across the state to a smaller, quieter town where housing prices were considerably lower. There we paid cash for a lovely four-bedroom house and still had money in the bank. The new house had everything we'd ever wanted in a home, including a huge family room. Shortly after moving there, as we were praying in that room, I envisioned it filled with people raising their hands and praising God. Although we experienced many wonderful "God things" in that house during the next seven years, we never saw the family room being used in that way. Nevertheless, I never forgot that mental picture.

God Sets up the Loom

In September 2011 Alan began experiencing shortness of breath. We'd had a very busy summer. In July we had commemorated our fiftieth anniversary with a five-day celebration that included a houseful of guests, travel, and a big dinner party. This was followed by entertaining a series of out-of-town guests, including our missionary friends from China. We attributed Alan's symptoms to all that extra activity and the hot, humid weather. But throughout the fall, his symptoms continued to come and go, so on the Sunday before Thanksgiving, Alan decided to get serious about attacking the problem. Being currently between churches, we attended a church in our town that we had visited occasionally where we knew they prayed for healing.

To our surprise, the regular pastor was gone and the associate pastor was leading the service. He spoke about the transition the church was about to go through. We learned later that the pastor had just resigned, leaving the congregation with no head pastor. After the service Alan went forward and asked for prayer for healing. He felt a new surge of energy and seemed to be breathing better. That same weekend in a small town south of Chicago, God spoke to a man named Pastor Jeff, telling him to begin preparing for transition. He was going to be moving, but God didn't say when or where.

We drove up to the Chicago area to spend Thanksgiving with our kids. Instead of improving, Alan's breathing problem escalated, so when we got home we sought medical help. Alan was diagnosed with a defective aortic valve. The heart specialist recommended surgery, but felt we could safely control the symptoms with medication until after the holidays. Alan's condition worsened. The angiogram on January 11 revealed he needed a lot more than a new valve; he also needed bypass surgery. Then, just three days later, the chest pains began, precipitating my call to the paramedics.

Parallel Threads

In January, on the western side of the state, we were dealing with angiograms, emergency helicopter rides, and heart surgery, while the church was dealing with the process of searching for a new pastor. At the same time, in a suburb north of Chicago, a young man named Alex was offered a fantastic opportunity for promotion on his job. This would entail moving with his wife and three-year-old daughter overseas for two years. He put his condo up for sale and began preparing for the move. And south of Chicago, Pastor Jeff and his wife were also preparing for their move, knowing that God had spoken, but having no clue as to when or where they would be going.

Every couple days, Pastor Paul or Darren from the church would drive forty-five miles to the hospital to visit and pray with us. The whole church had taken us on as a prayer project. When Pastor Darren came, he usually brought a team with him, and that was how I met a woman named Angie. Whenever she would visit, she would bring me a card with a very encouraging note.

On February 9, after Alan's first septic episode, I moved to the Family House. While living there, I got serious about seeking God, not for Alan's healing but for myself. I wanted closeness, intimacy, and an awareness of His presence. You already know that story.

Late in March, Alan died and I returned home. That first Sunday I didn't see Angie at church, but on Wednesday night I ran into her, and we talked in the lobby until it was time to go in for the service. We gradually became friends. At first I didn't realize she was married because, although she was at church every time the door opened, her husband never came.

Eventually I learned she did have a husband, but he was not a believer.

In April I came up to the north suburbs to find a home to rent. The housing market had slowed down a little by then, and Alex hadn't been able to sell his condo. On the other hand, the rental market was going like gangbusters, so he decided to lease it instead. And there I was, in the right place at the right time! I moved into the condo in early June, then my family and I returned to my house for one final garage sale and to pack up my stepmother's belongings and transport her to her new home near my condo.

When I returned with my stepmother in July, Angie came along to help me and to visit for a few days. One of our extended conversations was about her husband, Marty. Despite her praying for him for many years, he still hadn't accepted Jesus. Having observed how Alan and I interacted with each other in the hospital, she said she wanted her marriage to be like the one we had. I shared many things God had taught me about marriage, mainly about what I had learned regarding my attitude toward my husband based on 1 Peter 3:1-6. She went home with a new understanding of her priorities: her relationship with God first, then her relationship with Marty, and then the church and everyone else. As Marty noticed and responded to changes in her attitude toward him, their marriage began to improve.

Warp, Woof, and Waiting

I listed my house with a realtor, and in September he sold it with a contingency agreement, meaning the buyers were not obligated to complete the sale until they sold their house. Then the waiting began. For six months nothing happened. The church postponed their search for a new pastor in order to straighten out some problems and spruce up their property. Pastor Jeff and his wife continued to minister in their church as they waited to hear from God about their next step. My potential buyers waited for their house to sell.

As the months went by, I occasionally wondered why nothing was happening with my unoccupied house. Every six weeks I would renew my contract with the buyers, and we kept waiting for someone to come and buy their home. Although it seemed to be taking a long time, I wasn't worried. In fact, I was so busy that I didn't really give the house much thought most of the time. I had peace about the situation, believing God had a plan. I logically assumed His plan was that the buyers would eventually sell their house and complete the contract. That made sense, didn't it? But God had a better plan.

Spring arrived, and still there was no action. The realtor continued showing my house to prospective buyers, but the contingency seemed to be a hindrance. When one of my large trees fell across a fence into the neighbor's yard, the $450 removal cost served as a wake-up call. I realized the house was costing money, and as long as it was sitting unoccupied, it wasn't blessing anyone. I asked God if it was time to do something different about it. He gave me clear steps to follow – the first of which was not to renew the contract again, releasing me from any further obligation to the buyers.

That same week Pastor Jeff got a call from the district superintendent saying there was a church that really needed his expertise if he would be willing to come. Because God had already forewarned him, he was prepared to leave his very successful ministry, go where God had called him, and take on this new challenge. Angie called me with the news that the church was getting a new pastor, and he needed a house. She wanted my address. Although she passed the information along, somehow it never got to the pastor.

Not knowing this, I assumed the pastor wasn't interested in my house until one morning I felt God strongly impressing me to contact him directly. It turned out he had not found a place to live and hadn't heard about my house. He shared with me how God had told him months earlier to prepare for transition. When he got the call to this church he accepted immediately, even though there was no provision for housing. Obviously this was a true man of God who was willing to obey God first and ask questions later.

Pastor Jeff was at his computer during our conversation and wanted to know the address. When he pulled up the listing, he said, "Oh my! I know exactly where this is. When we drove by that house, my wife said that was the one she wanted, but we laughed because it wasn't in our price range." I told him since he was the pastor of the church that had blessed me so much, the price range would be different for him if he liked the house. He promised to have his realtor show it to him next time he was in town.

The Gift That Keeps on Giving

Two days later Pastor Jeff called back. "I'm sitting in front of your house right now. We just looked at it, and I am absolutely blown away! It is so beautiful!" He told me how perfect it would be for his family, then asked what price I had in mind. I was about to name an amount; it was on the tip of my tongue, when suddenly I found myself saying, "I believe God wants me to give that house to the church to use for a parsonage."

"Are you serious?" he asked.

"I guess I must be," I answered, although I was as surprised as he was! I told him all the ways that church had helped me during Alan's illness and after his death. The rest of our conversation was about how good and awesome God is.

When I hung up the phone, I had the distinct impression God was smiling at me. Alan had frequently said, "This isn't my house; it's God's house. If He told me to give it away, and I knew it was God, I would do it, just like that!" At the moment I wasn't thinking about what Alan always said, but I'm sure I did exactly what he would have done in the same situation.

After that, it was just a matter of some paperwork. It was really exciting to see how that one act of giving not only blessed the pastor, but energized the entire congregation of a church body that had been going through some very rough times. When Angie told Marty about it, he had a hard time understanding why someone would give away a perfectly good house. He had met me, and I had always seemed like a normal, sensible person. This was so out-of-the-box that it really caught his attention, giving Angie a chance to share financial principles from the Bible.

A few months later, God blessed Marty and Angie with an inheritance that enabled them to buy a house, something they had been wanting for years. Marty readily acknowledged that the inheritance and the house were blessings from God, and he had no problem giving away a portion of the inheritance money to help others. He had been seeing the goodness of God, and as Romans 2:4 says, *it is the goodness of God that leads men to repentance.*

Some of the men in the church had been reaching out to Marty, inviting him to do things with them, showing him God's unconditional love. Angie and Marty would get together with other couples from the church to play cards or share a meal. The guys, including Pastor Jeff, gathered on Sunday afternoons to watch football games. One day the pastor asked, "So Marty, when are we going to see you in church?"

"I'll tell you what," said Marty, "if you'll cheer for my team instead of yours, then I'll come to church." So the pastor made the "supreme sacrifice" and cheered for Marty's team, and the next Sunday Marty went to church. Apparently he liked it because he went again the next Sunday and the next. Soon Marty responded to an altar call and gave his life to Jesus.

And here's the exciting part. Guess where the men were gathering every Sunday to watch football! At my house! Nine years earlier, I had pictured the family room filled with people raising their hands in praise. I never saw it happen while we lived there, but it's happening now. That room is being used not only for watching football, but for all sorts of gatherings where God is being glorified, and it is frequently filled with people raising their hands and praising God.

Alan was right. That wasn't our house; it was God's. He had a plan for it all along. Angie had blessed me while Alan was in the hospital, and afterward as I was adjusting to life alone. Now my house played a part in bringing her husband into the kingdom of heaven, answering her prayers of many years. It's not uncommon for God to bring many paths across one another to bless a number of people with one situation, but usually we are only aware of our own part of the story. This time God graciously set things up so I could see how all of these crossing and connecting paths came together and how my almost-forgotten vision had come to pass. The crowning blessing was being at Marty's baptism service where I watched him propose to Angie, ring and all, asking her to renew their wedding vows!

Some people might call these parallel journeys and paths crossing at just the right moment coincidences, but I see the Master Planner's design running all through the tapestry. God loves setting up these situations. Consider the way He gave me a friend right next door. Einstein might have enjoyed calculating the odds of two newly singled-out women with similar circumstances winding up not just in the same building, but right next door to each other and moving in at practically the same time.

I don't think God chooses to remain anonymous. I think He enjoys hearing us tell people what He has done. I certainly don't believe He maneuvers us like puppets with no choice on our part, but when we make the choice to trust in Him and listen to His voice, He weaves things together perfectly, and we find ourselves in the right place at the right time. Then we look at the completed tapestry and simply marvel at His goodness and creativity.

The Journey Continues

This is not the end of my story. Threads are still being woven into the tapestry. Though I know more now about the destiny God has planned for me, He has not revealed exactly what the final picture will look like when it is completed. My journey as a singled-out woman so far has been an exciting adventure with a Traveling Companion who never ceases to amaze me with new evidences of His love, mercy, and grace.

Although I set foot on the path when I first began seeking Him diligently each morning, the journey really began when I made the commitment to trust Him no matter what. At that moment, His perfect love wiped away every trace of fear in my heart. When the worst possible thing I could imagine came to pass a week later, instead of falling apart I found peace and strength through my connection with Him. In the ensuing days He flooded me with supernatural joy and gave me Bible passages outlining the next step to take, and a hint at my future calling. As I continue the journey with Him, I find myself becoming more and more like the woman He created me to be. He has promised even more and better adventures ahead. I haven't arrived at my destination, but praise God I'm on my way and enjoying the trip!

The one whose mission is to steal, kill, and destroy managed to weasel his way into our lives, making Alan's last few months on earth very frightening and frustrating for all of us. I don't believe that was God's Plan A for the end of Alan's life. And when Alan died, this same enemy sought to destroy me as well by robbing me of my peace, joy, and strength. But fear, the weapon he previously used so effectively to cripple me in my spiritual walk, had been rendered powerless by my intimate relationship with God. I had experienced the love of God that surpasses all knowledge and the peace that passes all understanding. I was learning to establish my heart in my identity in Christ, and I was learning to stay my mind on Him. In His presence I found fullness of joy.

I'm no longer that frightened, spiritually timid woman who called 9-1-1. My inner man is *strong in the power of His might* (Ephesians 3:16). I face the future with confidence, and so can you. You can know firsthand the perfect love that demolishes all fear. As you embark on a serious walk with God, you will find not only precious intimacy, but you will discover peace in the midst of trials, joy in sorrowful circumstances, and strength to face whatever comes your way.

The First Step

The Christian life is a journey that begins with what Jesus called being born again. You are born again by receiving Jesus Christ as your Lord and Savior, which means you are making the choice to submit your life to him. Another name for this process is salvation. The good news is that God has already done everything necessary to provide for your salvation through Jesus' death on the cross. It's a free gift. You don't have to earn it; in fact, you can't!

Romans 10:9-10 promises *that if you confess with your mouth the Lord Jesus and believe in your heart that God has raised Him from the dead, you will be saved. For with the heart one believes unto righteousness, and with the mouth confession is made unto salvation.* And Romans 10:13 says, *For whoever calls on the name of the Lord shall be saved.*

Salvation is provided by God's grace. You receive it through faith, by believing in your heart, then confessing with your mouth by praying this prayer: "Jesus, I believe in my heart that You died on the cross for my sins, and that God raised you from the dead. I receive you as my Lord and Savior. According to Your Word in Romans 10:9-10 I'm now saved. I'm born again, my sins are forgiven, and my spirit is one with yours. Thank you, Jesus. Amen."

If you prayed this prayer and received Jesus, I would love to hear about it and send you additional information. Please visit my website at www.judyaknox.com and click on "Comments" at the top right of the screen, or write to me at Judy A. Knox, P.O. Box 873, Libertyville, IL 60048.

Resources

Establishing a Firm Foundation

The New You and the Holy Spirit, Andrew Wommack (Harrison House, Tulsa, OK 2012). The first part of the book explains salvation: why we need to be born again, how to be born again, and the results of being born again. The second part is about the baptism in the Holy Spirit: why we need it, how to receive it, and the results of receiving it. This book is given to each person who receives salvation or baptism in the Holy Spirit at Andrew Wommack's Gospel Truth Seminars.

Grace, the Power of the Gospel, Andrew Wommack (Harrison House, Tulsa, OK 2007). Based on the book of Romans, the author explains God's grace and how it operates in our lives as believers. If we understand Romans, we understand the gospel.

A Better Way to Pray, Andrew Wommack (Harrison House, Tulsa, OK 2007). A lot of the praying that we do as Christians is contrary to the way the Bible instructs us to pray. As a result, our prayer lives are not as effective as they could be. This book will help you pray more accurately and receive God's answers more quickly.

Understanding Who We Are in Christ

Spirit, Soul and Body, Andrew Wommack (Harrison House, Tulsa, OK 2010). More than any other book I know, this one clearly explains our new identity in Christ. We are made of three parts – spirit, soul, and body. When we are born again, our spirit is immediately changed, but our soul needs to be transformed by the renewing of our mind (Romans 12:2) and our body needs to be brought under subjection to our new identity. Understanding the truths in this book has revolutionized the lives of millions of Christians.

Destined to Reign, Joseph Prince (Harrison House, Tulsa, OK 2007). The primary message of this book is that living a victorious life is not about what we have to do, but what God has already done by sending Jesus to die on the cross. It helped me understand what Jesus really meant when He declared, "It is finished."

Quiet Time Helps

Jesus Calling: Enjoying Peace in His Presence, Sarah Young (Thomas Nelson, Nashville, TN 2011). This collection of 365 very short daily devotionals, written in first person as if God were writing it, was the book that first drew me into the presence of God. I don't agree 100 percent with the author's theology, but it is a great way to start your quiet time.

A Place of Quiet Rest: Finding Intimacy with God through a Daily Devotional Life, Nancy Leigh DeMoss (Moody Publishers, Chicago, IL 2002). This is a more in-depth discussion of why daily time with God is important and gives many suggestions for how to spend that time, as well as several good Bible-reading plans.

ABCs of Praise and Prayer: How 15 Minutes with God Can Change Your Day, Barbara Kois (Lighthouse Publishing of the Carolinas, Raleigh, NC 2013). Sometimes we just don't have time first thing in the morning for our Bible-reading plan. Here's a way to use your time in the car or sitting in a waiting room to focus your thoughts on God.

Books About Relationship and Intimacy with God

Relaxing with God: The Neglected Spiritual Discipline, Andrew Farley (Baker Books, Grand Rapids, MI 2014). This book was a delightful surprise. Expecting to be told about the importance of spending time with God, I learned instead to get out of works-based religion and into the freedom of God's grace.

Having a Mary Heart in a Martha World: Finding Intimacy with God in the Busyness of Life, Joanna Weaver (WaterBrook Press, Colorado Springs, CO 2009). The title perfectly describes the book. I read this book years before becoming a widow. It is fun to read and brimming with good stories from the author's life and great Bible-based teaching.

A Shepherd Looks at Psalm 23, Phillip Keller (Zondervan, Grand Rapids, MI 2007). God used the relationship between shepherd and sheep many places in the Bible. Here, a real life shepherd explains what all the analogies and word pictures in the 23rd Psalm mean. After reading this book, you will have a better understanding of how much God loves you and cares for you.

Song of Songs: Divine Romance, The Passion Translation, Dr. Brian Simmons (BroadStreet Publishing Group, Racine, WI 2014). Many books of the Bible have been published in the Passion Translation. This one is my favorite, a depiction of God's love for us in twenty-first century language that is easy to understand and envision. Be sure to read the author's introduction first.

Hosting the Presence: Unveiling Heaven's Agenda, Bill Johnson (Destiny Image Publishers, Inc., Shippensburg, PA 2012). All of us, as believers, have the Holy Spirit dwelling in us, but truly experiencing His presence does not come automatically. We must choose to host the presence in our lives, and this book shows us how.

Enjoying the Presence of God: Discovering Intimacy with God in the Daily Rhythms of Life, Jan Johnson (NavPress, Colorado Springs, CO 1996). If you have viewed spending time with God as a chore or performance, this book, based on Brother Lawrence's classic book, *Practicing the Presence of God,* will help you surrender to His presence and enjoy just being with Him.

Simple Faith: How Every Person Can Experience Intimacy with God, Eddie Snipes (Exchanged Life Publishing, 2013). The author uses parable-like stories to illustrate scriptural principles and teaches about the simplicity of the gospel and the Bible. The book is easy to read and understand.

Winning the Spiritual Battles

Angels: Knowing Their Purpose, Releasing Their Power, Charles and Annette Capps (Capps Publishing, England, AR 1994). A look at the subject of angels from a biblical perspective, this is the book that taught me how speaking Scripture will release angels into the situation. It also explains many other reasons why it is important to watch our words.

"Massive Stroke – Healed" http://www.awmi.net/extra/healing/moore. This awesome testimony shows how one couple was able to be spiritually minded, as I talk about in Chapter 9: Words, Thoughts, and Deeds despite the circumstances, including doctors' reports. As a result, the husband received a miraculous healing.

"Power of Faith-filled Words" http://www.awmi.net/extra/article/power_faith This online article gives more details about how our words affect our world. On the page with the article are further resources available on the topic, and many are free.

Books for Widows

Singled Out for God's Assignment: A Widow's Valley of Learning, Leona Choy (Golden Morning Publishers, Winchester, VA 1996). This was the first book I read about widowhood after losing my husband, and it was practical as well as encouraging. I especially love the title. It put my new road ahead into God's perspective.

From One Widow to Another: Conversations on the New You, Marian Neff (Moody Publishers, Chicago, IL 2009). This is another very practical, helpful book for a woman who suddenly finds herself one person instead of half of a couple. The author also has a website and other resources for Christian widows.

Other Helpful Materials

Heaven is for Real, Todd Burpo (Thomas Nelson, Nashville, TN 2011). This best-selling true story about a little boy who went to heaven and met Jesus was not only pleasant and heart-warming to read, it was further confirmation to me of the reality of where Alan is now. It offers encouragement for anyone who has lost a loved one.

Psalms: Poetry on Fire, The Passion Translation, Dr. Brian Simmons (BroadStreet Publishing Group, Racine, WI 2014). The Passion Translation is not a substitute for other versions, but it is like reading the Bible and a commentary all in one. This will enhance your appreciation of the Psalms and makes great bedtime reading.

Financial Breakthrough – Judy Knox http://www.awmi.net/extra/financial/knox This is the testimony I shared on television about how Alan and I sold our house in two days without a realtor, as I shared in Chapter 4: "Hearing God's Voice."

About the Author

Judy Knox, a retired high school teacher, now teaches Christians how to get more from their relationship with God. Recently widowed, she resides most of the year in northern Illinois near her married son and daughter and six grandchildren, and flies south to Arizona for the winter months. Judy is the author of *Dewdrops of Grace*, a collection of devotionals. In addition to writing and speaking, she is active in her local church and enjoys playing the cello.

Contact Information

Website and Blog: www.judyaknox.com Newsletter and Blog sign-up forms are at the top of the page on full-screen version, after the posts on the mobile version.

Facebook Author Page: https://www.facebook.com/ JudyAKnoxAuthor (Search Judy A. Knox)

CPSIA information can be obtained
at www.ICGtesting.com
Printed in the USA
FFOW04n2006050116
19981FF

9 781622 453160